ADOGA

A Science and Spirituality of Profound Patterns

by
Ryan Taylor

Second Edition

© 2020 Ryan Taylor

First edition published 2020. Second edition published 2023.

All rights reserved. No portion of this book may be reproduced in any form without permission from the publisher, except as permitted by U.S. copyright law.

Request permissions at: contact@projectado.com
www.projectado.com

ISBN: 978-1-7324819-7-8

The day science begins to study non-physical phenomena, it will make more progress in one decade than in all the previous centuries of its existence.

-Nikola Tesla

Contents
Condensed

Introduction • 8

Part I – The Journey to Oneness
Chapter One – Subtle Energy and Foundational Practices • 18
Chapter Two – Breath and Release • 33
Chapter Three – Oneness and the Ado • 39

Part II – The Four Trees of Adoga
Chapter Four – The Tree of Practices • 66
Chapter Five – The Tree of Rest • 92
Chapter Six – The Tree of Emotions • 98
Chapter Seven – The Tree of Thoughts • 114

Part III – Methods and Expansions
Chapter Eight – The Methods of Adoga • 136
Chapter Nine – Expansions • 155

Conclusion
Imagining the World Anew • 171
Appendix 1 – A Map of the Ado Tree • 175
Appendix 2 – Yin, Yang, and the Elemental Archetypes • 181
Acknowledgments • 184
Bibliography • 188
Index • 191

Contents
Expanded

Introduction • 8
What Is Adoga and What Does It Offer? • 8
Self-Acceptance and Self-Growth • 10
The Importance of Self-Growth • 11
The Journey From Many to One and From One Back to Many • 13
A Short Summary • 15

Part I
The Journey to Oneness

Chapter One – Subtle Energy and Foundational Practices • 18
The Duality of Yune and Kav • 18
Subtle Energy • 21
Foundational Practices • 25
Relax and Release • 26
Grounding • 27
Connecting to Heaven • 28
Observing the Centers and the Breath • 28
Creating Love and Gratitude • 30

Chapter Two – Breath and Release • 33
What Does It Mean to Cry? • 34
A Societal Shift Surrounding Emotional-Spiritual Expression • 36
Physical Manifestations of Release (PMRs) in Adoga • 37
Other Physical Manifestations of Release (PMRs) • 38

Chapter Three – Oneness and the Ado • 39
What Are Thoughts? • 40
Oneness • 43
Form, Holan, and Energy • 45
The Principle of Infinite Potential • 48
The World of the Ado • 54
New Words • 56
Tree Language • 58

Part II
The Four Trees of Adoga

Chapter Four – The Tree of Practices • 66
An Introduction to Intentions • 68
Receive (Yune 1) • 69
Create (Kav 2) • 73
The Method of Discovering Ados • 74
Observe (Yunor 1.2) • 75
Feel (Yunem 1.1) • 78
Imagine (Kavek 2.1) • 80
Intend (Kavos 2.2) • 86
Receiving and Creating Revisited • 88
Adoga Practices from Yune to Kav • 89
Cultivating the Practices • 90

Chapter Five – The Tree of Rest • 92

Release Intention (Kav 2) • 95

Release Consciousness (Yune 1) • 95

Release Direct Intention and Immediate Goals (Kavos 2.2) • 96

Release Imagination, Fixation, and Larger Goals (Kavek 2.1) • 96

Release Observation and Inner Divisions (Yunor 1.2) • 97

Release Foundational Energies (Yunem 1.1) • 97

Chapter Six – The Tree of Emotions • 98

Hurt-Love (Yunes 1.1.1) and Hate-Joy (Yunet 1.1.2) • 102

Depression-Peace (Yunov 1.2.1) and Grief-Appreciation (Yunoj 1.2.2) • 104

Fear-Excitement (Kaves 2.1.1) and Attachment-Inspiration (Kavel 2.1.2) • 109

Anger-Power (Kavoj 2.2.1) and Frustration-Satisfaction (Kavov 2.2.2) • 112

Chapter Seven – The Tree of Thoughts • 114

Essence and Identity (Yunem 1.1) • 116

Freedom and Possibility (Yunor 1.2) • 123

Purpose and Clarity (Kavek 2.1) • 125

Focus and Resonance (Kavos 2.2) • 127

A Summary of the Four Trees of Adoga • 132

Part III
Methods and Expansions

Chapter Eight – The Methods of Adoga • 136
Alignment Method: Aligning State With Practice • 136
Symmetry Method: The Mysterious Relationships of Symmetry • 140
Symmetrical Cycles of Growth • 144
Aligning Practice With Potential Energy • 146
Flexible and Fixed Intention • 148
Learning Adoga in Stages • 150
The Process of a Dedicated Session • 152

Chapter Nine – Expansions • 155
Practicing Adoga in Day-to-Day Life • 155
Execution and Discovery • 156
Practices on the Eight-Part Level of Division • 160
A Mental Discovery System • 165
Relational Adoga • 168

Conclusion • 171
Imagining the World Anew • 171
Appendix 1: A Map of the Ado Tree • 175
Appendix 2: Yin, Yang, and the Elemental Archetypes • 181
Acknowledgments • 184
Bibliography • 188
Index • 191

Introduction

What Is Adoga and What Does It Offer?

Adoga is something mysterious. Something beautiful. Powerful. Complex. Something that could change the world. Something that could change your life.

Its description runs deeply throughout the structure of the universe. It is something that we will define in progressively unfolding layers. Our first definition is this: Adoga is a system and practice of self-growth inspired by big-picture patterns or archetypes – specifically the biggest-picture patterns that our minds can comprehend.

The focus of Adoga is the improvement of one's *emotional-spiritual state*. The emotional-spiritual state is the summation of one's emotions, awareness, spiritual perception, felt sensation, and general experience arising in the present moment. This state forms a foundation that has the power to support or inhibit the quality of your thoughts, actions, and results.

Adoga moves its practitioners toward an exciting reality: one where emotions and states are intelligent informants and intentional creations that act as resources for one's goals. With practice, one can achieve access to an immense diversity of positive states to explore: joyful passion, ecstatic pleasure, the relief of peace, a sense of oneness or connectivity with the world, awareness of incredible complexity, awe, a sense of being integrated and whole, or a purposeful dedication that seems to permeate one's whole being down to the bones. Not only are states fun to explore, they are also profoundly useful, life-changing in fact. What if your mind felt activated, intuitive, and fruitful in a situation that called for your creativity? What if you could stay connected to yourself and others during that difficult conversation? What if you could calm your anxiety at will? What if you had energy when you needed it most? When you have access to the emotions and states you desire, you can act from those places producing – sometimes dramatically – different results in your life.

While developing empowering states, the practitioner of Adoga also receives another, more subtle, benefit. Healing the negative aspects of our inner worlds and cultivating positive states naturally creates the byproduct of wisdom and insight. While we may have desires for our state, we will also find that our state has desires for us. Our emotions are like messengers. They all have something to say, and they will generally persist until they are satisfied that they have been listened to. The more we cultivate the capacity to lovingly listen to ourselves, the more we will hear the wisdom our state has to offer. This is not to say that the voice of our state will always be a wise one. Rather, it is to say that the more we cultivate the ability to listen, the more truth we will hear.

The goal of Adoga then is the formation of an individual of both power and loving wisdom, and this is accomplished through the transformation of one's inner state. This transformation, while challenging at times, is rewarding, meaningful, and wonderfully joyful in its attainment.

Self-Acceptance and Self-Growth

Self-acceptance, self-love, and self-forgiveness are common themes in psychology and spirituality. By letting go of our shame, we can remove limitations that we previously imposed on ourselves.

Is this principle of self-acceptance in conflict with the principle of self-growth or self-development? After all, one seems to point to the idea that you are perfect the way you are, whereas the other seems to indicate the necessity of changing yourself. I believe there is no contradiction between the two principles and that both have valuable contributions to offer, but to see this, we must understand each principle properly.

Self-growth refers to the improvement of a person's attributes: their skills, knowledge, awareness, values, perspectives, emotional fortitude, intelligence, and so on. Self-love, on the other hand, refers to the acceptance of a person's essence: their good intent, their journey, their spiritual essence, their personhood. It is possible to critique a person's attributes in a loving manner rather than a hateful one. It is the emotion behind the critique that determines if it will be the source of destructive shame or the source of genuinely motivated self-growth.

Furthermore, we can critique a person's attributes without judging the person as essentially, permanently, and fundamentally bad. The judgment of a person as fundamentally bad is the source of shame and is inherently destructive. Attributes can be differentiated from personhood, allowing traits to be evaluated and improved while the person at an essential level remains loved and accepted.

The ultimate aim, then, is to realize a way of being in the world that is loving and forgiving, yet can also passionately and effectively fight for personal and societal improvement. In this sense, Adoga is not only a system of self-growth but also a system of self-acceptance or self-love.

Adoga honors both loving forgiveness and inspirational passion. With both principles intertwined into a single thread of living and becoming, we can find ourselves and elevate ourselves at the same time.

The Importance of Self-Growth

Some object to self-growth, spirituality, philosophy, and intense intellectualization because they feel it lacks practical application. Adoga involves all those areas, so I should emphasize that the practical application is very real and very important. Although the transformation of self-growth begins internally, in the end it affects those around us and the world at large.

We can think about it this way: Self-growth is like

the development of a set of tools and resources. Let's say I ask two people to traverse a thousand miles as quickly as possible. One person is given shoes, a water bottle, and a backpack in terms of tools and resources. The other person is given an airplane, an experienced pilot, and a runway at either end of the trip. If we were to have these two race against one another, who do you expect would win?

Better tools produce better results. And sometimes the difference is profound. Tools and resources come in many forms, but *you* – your own *self* – is the first and most important tool that you'll ever have. It is the only tool that you can always count on having access to. It is the tool you have the most control over. Developing your *self*, your most important and central resource, is not only worthwhile but of the utmost importance.

Self-growth is not selfish. It is not just about you. We can contribute more to the world when we work on our own tool set. Self-growth is not about things that are merely "nice to have." I believe that it is a *crucial* part of what is *required* for the world to move forward.

However, there is a balance to strike here: the balance between short-term and long-term gain. We can't spend so long on developing tools that our short-term needs go unmet. A civilization only capable of hiking cannot stop all travel to focus on the development of airplanes. Such a civilization would not be able to meet their short-term needs and would fail to construct an airplane as a result. The lesson here is that when possible, long-term strategies can have a tremendous advantage.

Though, they must be kept in balance.

Self-growth is a long-term strategy, the equivalent of building an airplane. It has great benefit, but it takes time and energy. The recommendation, then, is to put as much effort into self-growth as is reasonable and possible for you, committing yourself to it as inspiration strikes, yet avoiding the sacrifice of immediate needs.

The Journey From Many to One and From One Back to Many

Much of spirituality is oriented around the journey from the many to the one. This journey starts with a fragmented, lonely, perhaps even competitive or violent self and ends with a self that is connected to something bigger. It ends with a self that finds its connection to or even its definition in universality, oneness, spirit, God – these are some of the many words that point to an essential, omnipresent reality. The journey from the many to the one reveals the important truth that some inherent substrate is shared among all things.

Adoga builds upon the foundation of the journey to oneness. Perceiving a unified reality, Adoga asks, "How does oneness give rise to multiplicity?" It asks, "How does the universe first break apart? What are its fundamental parts? What are the first pieces of the many? And how do the first pieces of the many give rise to the later parts?" Thus, Adoga is the spiritual journey from the one to the many.

The premise of oneness and its fundamental parts enables the creation of highly encompassing perspectives, and this is where much of the significance and power of Adoga is derived. Encompassing perspectives allow us to see a broader and deeper perception of the world. A primary strategy for creating encompassing perspectives is to discover views that seem to oppose each other and yet both contain an element of truth. In such opposing perspectives, we can find integrations and harmonies between radically different understandings of the world.

Encompassing perspectives are important on several fronts. They help eliminate blind spots, which are areas that fall outside our awareness or that have biases imposed against them. They help eliminate conflict-ridden divides, which pit one half of the truth against the other half. They give us access to a larger spectrum of awareness and choices, when otherwise we might be stuck in narrow habits and viewpoints.

We have already introduced a couple of these integrations. We combined the ideas of self-acceptance and self-growth. We also considered the need to balance short-term and long-term strategies. In both cases, we found that the opposing principles revealed different aspects of the truth but did not contradict each other when we considered them carefully. By understanding both sides of the truth and resolving any apparent contradictions, we were able to form a higher, more encompassing perspective.

Another integration that is featured prominently in

Adoga is the inclusion of both science and spirituality. In other words, Adoga integrates the intellectual with the emotional. Adoga is a science of spirituality. It is a rigorous, complex, testable, and challengeable framework that attempts to map the emotional and spiritual experience.

These deep ways of understanding the world are profoundly important. They allow us to perceive true purpose, rather than wallowing in the chaos of distraction, shallow pleasure, and poverty disguised as wealth. They allow us to come home to ourselves without discomfort but instead with a visceral knowing of life's great meaning and beauty. Traveling toward greater depth, we embark on a truly exciting journey, one of tremendous potency, potential, and significance.

A Short Summary

Briefly, let's take a look at what this journey has in store for us. We will begin by creating a foundation in the theory and practice of the *many to one* spiritual journey. In this first part of the book, we will learn how to experience and understand oneness. Along the way, we will introduce some of the most fundamental concepts of Adoga as well as some foundational self-growth concepts and practices, including the subtle energies of the body and physical pathways for emotional release.

In Part Two, we will begin the journey of *one to many spirituality*. Here we will discover the paradigm of Adoga organized into four "trees" or systems, each focused on a different context: practices, rest, emotions, and thoughts.

Part Three interrelates these four trees into a unified whole. The core power of Adoga is found in the relationships within and between the four trees, which show how specific emotions relate to specific practices, how specific mindsets are supported by different emotional states, how emotional states relate to each other, and many other illuminating connections. Here we will discover how the trees of emotions and thoughts inform how we use the trees of practice and rest. We will also briefly touch upon a few expansions to the core Adoga framework.

This book has two appendices. The first is a map of all four trees of Adoga and their many associations, which are presented throughout the book. This may be a useful reference as you are reading. The second appendix briefly discusses the relationship of Adoga to the ancient concept of yin and yang and to systems of elemental archetypes like the *I Ching*.

While exploring this vast territory of subjects, we will build up a self-growth practice of increasing depth and complexity. I highly recommend developing your skill with the practices as they are presented. In this way, you can synergistically develop your theoretical understanding and practical skillset together.

With much gratitude for your interest, I welcome you to this inspiring, beautiful, and powerful world. I invite you to explore with joy.

Part I

The Journey to Oneness

Chapter One
Subtle Energy and Foundational Practices

The Duality of Yune and Kav

Adoga is a landscape and world unto itself. It requires a unique language for its description. I will introduce many new words on our journey, some of which have been created specifically for their purpose in the Adoga system. To begin our journey, we will explore two such words: *yune* and *kav*. These two words represent two opposing sets of qualities. Throughout this book we will explore the spectrum created between these two polarities. Adoga is largely based on the foundation of this spectrum.

Both yune and kav are conglomerations and integrations of a diverse array of associations. Yune is associated with unity, generality, receptivity, and potential. Kav is the opposing principle, defined by associations with multiplicity, specificity, expression, and manifestation.

Unification produces things that encompass more of the universe, things that are more general. Division produces increasing levels of multiplicity, things that encompass less, and things that are more specific. Therefore, yune is associated with generality and unification, while kav is associated with specificity and division.

When we become more receptive, we become open to a greater array of possibilities. In contrast, expression represents the act of choosing a limited set of possibilities to create. Therefore, receptivity is the personal movement toward generality and unity, while expression is the personal movement toward specificity and multiplicity. For this reason, yune is receptive, whereas kav is expressive.

Receptivity leads inward and toward the self. It also leads to greater awareness. Yune, then, inherits these associations as well: inwardness, self, and awareness. Expression projects outward, toward the external world. It requires the active use of will, or in other words, intention. Therefore, kav is associated with outwardness, the world, and intention. The use of intention creates activity and requires balance with rest. Kav is associated with activity, whereas yune is associated with rest.

Yune is associated with *causal principles* that influence many events and thus are general in nature. Kav is associated with the individual *manifestations* of such causal principles. For example, in a relationship, many arguments may occur, which on the surface appear to be about different topics. However, perhaps every argument was most fundamentally caused by an inability to listen to the other person. In this example, the causal principle would be the inability to listen, and each individual argument could be thought of as a manifestation of that causal principle. Causal principles may be enacted in different ways and they can exist while not being enacted or expressed in a particular moment of time. In this way, causal principles are forms of potential. Therefore, yune is associated with potentiality, while kav is associated with the realization or manifestation of that potential.

The early stages of any endeavor involve receptivity, learning, and opening up to possibilities. As the endeavor progresses, possibilities will be investigated, narrowed down, and finally specific possibilities will be selected as components of the final product. Therefore, yune is associated with beginnings, while kav is associated with endings.

The table below summarizes all of these associations:

Yune	Kav
Unity	Multiplicity
Generality	Specificity
Receptivity	Expression
Inwardness	Outwardness
Self	World
Awareness	Intention
Rest	Activity
Causal Principles	Manifestations of Causal Principles
Potential	Manifestation
Beginnings	Endings

Subtle Energy

Energy is an aspect of all things. It describes something about everything, especially that ability to work, move, and create change. *Subtle energy* is the substance and potential for work that inhabits the emotional, mental, and spiritual realms. In contrast, what we could call *dense energy* inhabits the physical and manifested realm. I describe this kind of energy as dense because it has greater momentum. Once in a particular configuration, dense energy likes to stay in that configuration for a while. Subtle energy, in contrast, changes form more easily. For example, how long does it take you to create a tea cup in your imagination? How long does it take you to create the same tea cup in physical or manifested reality? You can create the tea cup in your mind more quickly because subtle energy is easier to reconfigure. The tea cup in your mind is also more subtle in the sense that its qualities are less defined and more malleable and therefore more difficult to perceive with certainty.

Donna Eden provides the following context about subtle energy in her book *Energy Medicine*:

Numerous cultures describe a matrix of subtle energies that support, shape, and animate the physical body, often displaying intelligence that transcends human knowing, called qi *or* chi *in China,* prana *in the yoga tradition of India and Tibet,* ruach *in Hebrew,* ki *in Japan,* baraka *by the Sufis,* wakan *by the Lakotas,* orenda *by the Iroquois,* megbe *by the Ituri Pygmies, and the* Holy Spirit *in Christian tradition. It is hardly a new idea to suggest that subtle energies operate in tandem with the denser, "congealed" energies of the material body.*

Throughout the rest of her book, Donna Eden goes on to describe a detailed and complex map of subtle energies, frequently referring to emerging science that supports and parallels the knowledge of the spiritual traditions. And indeed, every spiritual tradition seems to have their own way of describing and categorizing these phenomena.

For our purposes, we will focus on a relatively simple map of subtle energies, comprising just a few elements that are common across many systems. To start with, I'll present a few *centers* of subtle energy in the human body. The following insights of Christopher Wallis, teacher of meditation, yoga, and Tantrik philosophy, are helpful here:

The energy body (sūkshma-sharīra) is an extraordinarily fluid reality, as we should expect of anything nonphysical and supersensuous. The energy body can present, experientially speaking, with any number of energy centers, depending on the person and the yogic practice they're performing.

Having said that, there are a few centers which are found in all systems: specifically, in the lower belly or sexual center, in the heart, and in or near the crown of the head, since these are three places in the body where humans all over the world experience both emotional and spiritual phenomena.

Author Frederic Laloux offers a more biological perspective of the same reality:

How many brains does a human being have? I imagine your answer is "one" (or, if you suspected a trick question, it might be "two," the often-referred-to right and left brains). Our current knowledge is that we have three: there is of course the massive brain in our head; then there is a small brain in our heart, and another in our gut. The last two are comparatively much smaller, but they are fully autonomous nervous systems nevertheless.

Note that no remarkable belief in subtle energy is required to begin developing your emotional-spiritual state through self-growth practice. Although science offers fascinating and illuminating connections to subtle energy, the ultimate reality we are describing here is subjective. At its simplest level, if you experience the sensation of emotion, if you experience the subjective sense of awareness, then you are experiencing subtle energy. Centers of subtle energy refer to common experiences in this realm around certain areas of the body.

The three centers, in the belly, heart, and head, form a column or channel of subtle energy from the pelvis up to the top of the head. Let's briefly examine each center:

We can think of the *gut center* as occupying the physical territory throughout the belly and solar plexus area, all the way down to the base of the spine. This center is associated with survival, safety, stability, and sexuality. This is the center that connects us to the earth, to the ancestors, and to our earlier development as individuals and as a society. This is the foundation or root of the energetic system. The common sayings "He's got guts!" or "She had a gut feeling," are also illuminating associations, revealing connections to bravery and a certain flavor of intuition, respectively.

Next is the *heart center*, located around the chest, lungs, and, of course, heart. This center is associated with emotion, passion, love, and relationship. I think of the heart as the primary center of emotional-spiritual energy. It plays a powerful role in governing all emotions: hurt, numbness, and anger, as well as joy, love, and inspiration. The heart center is also the most central of the centers. It is in the middle of the three centers we are describing here and, thus, also takes on the function of unifying, balancing, and integrating the forces of the lower energies with the forces of the higher energies.

Lastly, we can turn our attention to the *head center*. The head center is associated with both intellect and spirit. The common expression of "being heady" is descriptive. This is the center that allows for higher levels of abstraction. It is the home of both defined thought and fluid, mind-oriented intuition. This is the center that creates the processes of observation and imagination. It is also the place where we can access spiritual experiences of transcendence and ego-dissolution. The head center allows us to contemplate a large space of possibilities: potentials for the future, ideals, principles, and generalities.

Now, we have a picture of three centers – gut, heart,

and head – forming a column of energy in the body. I will add just one additional element to this map: *breath*. Breath, like the three centers, is also a common component of diverse spiritual systems and self-growth methods. I see the breath as the primary mover of subtle energies. Exhale is an important mechanism for release and inhale for the reception of nourishing energies. I associate the breath with movement, balance, cyclical motion, and transformation.

The map we have laid out is a simple picture of a complex reality. However, in that simplicity lies a great power. By working with just these four elements – gut, heart, head, and breath – we can quickly access the most important aspects of subtle energy in the body.

Foundational Practices

Now, I'll introduce a set of foundational self-growth practices that act on the map of subtle energies we have constructed. You can go far with just these foundational practices. I invite you to take as long as you need to become familiar with these fundamentals and integrate them into your day-to-day experience before moving on to the practices I present later on.

Relax and Release

This first practice, named relax and release, is a component of all other practices we will discuss. It is the foundation of the foundation. This is the mechanism through which the old can be let go of thus creating potential for the new. A key insight of the relax and release practice is that we can *release* – that is eliminate unhealthy elements of the emotional-spiritual state – by *relaxing*.

To practice relaxing and releasing means to cease expenditure of effort – perhaps exempting efforts needed for practical functions like the effort to remain upright if you happen to be in a seated position. In relaxation, our goals and intentions melt away and are replaced by potentiality. It can be comforting to know that your goals and intentions need only be let go of for the time being; you can always bring them back. But in the moments when you are relaxing, there is no goal, no objective, no better direction, no worse direction.

Practiced powerfully, relaxing and releasing creates a movement of subtle energy throughout the body, as old energies leave, creating space for new ones. The process of release naturally moves us to exhale deeply. If this urge arises, the invitation is to allow the body to breathe as it wants to.

Relaxing and releasing is key for creating potential energy that can be used in any other practice. Any practice that creates new subtle energies will also use release to dispel any energy that is not compatible with the new energies you are creating. So it is good to always have a piece of your awareness be a steward of the releasing process, facilitating the departure of that which no longer serves you.

Grounding

Grounding is important for facilitating balance and a foundation of resource and readiness. It also provides a connection and harmony between the inner and outer worlds, which strengthens the manifestation of new causal principles you can develop in other practices.

To practice grounding, focus your attention on the earth, perhaps starting with the ground directly beneath you and deepening into the earth as far as you want to go. With your attention on the earth, imagine any energies that no longer serve you dissipating into the ground. Imagine anything that is in excess coming into balance. Now, invite the earth to support you by giving you energy from its abundant reserves. Imagine anything that is deficient coming into balance.

This process can be summarized by two central intentions: connect to the earth and facilitate balance. If you have grounded successfully, you should feel a sense of stability, calm, and readiness. This practice can be made more powerful by standing barefoot on a piece of natural ground.

Connecting to Heaven

This is a complementary practice to grounding and works well following a grounding practice. To connect to heavenly energies, focus your attention on the sky. Reflect upon and take in the sky's light, its spaciousness, the way it frames and holds all the creativity of the world below it. Imagine any energies that are ready to leave flowing up and out of your body into the heavens, dissipating into potential as they do so. Invite the sky to support you by giving you energy from its abundant reserves. Feel or imagine feeling the energy of the sun on your skin. As with grounding, this practice can be more powerful in nature.

Observing the Centers and the Breath

Awareness is key. Observing increases awareness. To know how our energy centers are doing in each moment makes us aware of knowledge that is important for our self-growth and for our decision-making. In addition, emotions are like messengers who speak more and more loudly until they are listened to. Therefore, the practice of listening to emotions (or other energetic experiences) satisfies the emotions and calms them. Listening allows emotions to do their natural job. Listening does not mean that you should believe or act on every emotional message you receive. Listening means only that you hold compassionate and receptive space, taking in what you want to hold on to and letting go of whatever wants to be released. On account of its receptive nature, this practice is associated with yune.

To practice observation, notice what sensations, feelings, and experiences are happening within yourself in the present moment. You may choose to focus this observation on one of the three centers or the breath. You may also choose to keep the observation receptive to the entirety of your subtle energy field.

Regardless of the focus, stay with the experience in the present moment and refrain from investing in thoughts, stories, explanations, and imaginations. If thoughts arise, simply notice them and return your attention to object of your focus. Continually renew your sense of receptivity, openness, and curiosity. Ask repeatedly, "What is emerging *now*?" And each time, ask with the knowledge that you do not know the answer to your question. Each time, ask with an emotion of love, care, and connection, as if you are talking to a good friend about something important to both of you.

As you receive, allow whatever wants to be released to be released. Allow exhale to carry you forward.

I recommend becoming familiar with this practice first with the breath, then with the heart center, then with the head center, and finally with the gut center. Once you are comfortable observing each of these individually, you can try observing each in turn during a single meditation, perhaps starting with the breath and then going through each of the centers from bottom to top. With more experience, you can also try observing your entire energetic system at once. You may find it helpful in this last variation to allow your focus to go to whatever aspect of the energy system feels most in need of attention.

Creating Love and Gratitude

We often think of emotions as being caused by our external life conditions. However, just as much as emotions are responses, they are internal creations produced by our thoughts, intentions, and focus.

By focusing on an emotion and directing energy to it, you can manifest the object of your focus. This is the essential kav practice, the expressive polarity of working with emotional-spiritual states.

The following practice is a technique for the creation of the emotional-spiritual state of love, perhaps the most foundational of positive energies. Imagine a situation where you feel love: perhaps, playing with an animal or looking into a child's eyes. To start with, use an imagination that is uncomplicated and powerful. As you imagine the loving situation, draw your attention to how you would feel in this situation. Move from imagining the externals of the situation to imagining the internal emotional and energetic experience. Notice what you do within yourself in this state. You may notice that through this process, your imagination manifests into present moment experience: physical sensations, emotions, and awareness. You can invite this manifesting process to actualize and deepen.

As new subtle energies manifest, allow anything that is not compatible to be released. You might naturally find yourself in a cycle of creating and releasing, creating and releasing.

After creating new love energy within yourself, you can perform different variations on this practice. You can try bringing this new loving energy into imaginations where it is more difficult for you to feel love. You might, for example, think of a person in your life who you have a strained relationship with and imagine sending them love and compassion. You can also expand the energy of love within yourself by sending it out to people you don't know, to countries, planets, abstractions, and anything else you can conjure up!

You can try variations of this practice with other positive feelings like joy, peace, or enthusiasm. Gratitude is also a particularly foundational and important energy to cultivate. To create the energy of gratitude within yourself, bring into your imagination things you appreciate or things that fill you with a sense of awe and wonder. You can think of simple things like the smile on a stranger's face or you can think of grand things like the mysteries of science, the vastness of space and time, the beauty of your favorite piece of art, or the divinity of your favorite slice of nature. In all of these possibilities, intend to sensitize yourself to what is good in life. Take a moment to reflect on what you like and what creates positive emotion for you. The more you bring energy to the things you like in your internal sphere, the more you will notice them externally, the more you will create them (consciously and subconsciously), and, ultimately, the more you will facilitate their manifestation in your life.

Chapter Two
Breath and Release

When the emotional-spiritual state changes, corresponding effects in the physical body are produced. Most prominently, we see the physical body react to the *release* of emotional-spiritual energies. In my experience, the creation of new emotional-spiritual energy also creates parallel changes in the physical body; though, these tend to be more subtle.

Release, manifest in the physical body, often looks like *crying, laughing,* or *sighing*. I describe these kinds of behaviors as *physical manifestations of release*, or *PMRs* for short.

These three primary PMRs – crying, laughing, and sighing – share similarities. First of all, they all involve the breath (which we defined in the last chapter as the primary mover of subtle energy). Crying and laughing are both forms of *pulsating breath.* In normal breathing, we inhale and then exhale in a smooth progression from one to the other and back again. In crying and laughing, we exhale, stop, exhale, stop, and so on… then inhale. For crying, the pattern tends to be pulsating exhaling following by a single, big inhale. Laughing changes slightly in that the pulsation may continue into the inhale.

These pulsating breathing patterns seem to result from emotional-spiritual changes that are felt to be particularly pronounced or dramatic by the body. The *sigh* or emphasized exhale is more subtle, though often very significant. The scale of an emotional-spiritual change does not always correlate to the scale of the accompanying PMR. We can make a life-changing alteration to our perspective, and all that comes physically is a gentle exhale. In comparison, even a physically intense bout of crying could potentially be the product of a lesser shift in emotional-spiritual terms.

What Does It Mean to Cry?

Interpreting crying as a PMR is a radical change in perspective, relative to the modern, standard perception of crying. The standard interpretation of today's culture – at least as far as I've seen – is that crying is a sign that someone is sad or in a negative emotional-spiritual state. Interpreting crying as a PMR, in contrast, connects crying to release or the *change* of one's state from one place to another. Release is a natural process, guided by natural wisdom. Generally, PMRs do not occur unless something that needs to be released is being released. Therefore, it is usually safe to assume that as long as a PMR is genuine, *it is a beneficial process* for the person experiencing the release. In some cases, it may be *extremely* beneficial.

Really when you see someone crying, you should be happy for them. This is not to say that you should be insensitive either. Crying is still often a difficult experience, even if it is beneficial. But there are many experiences that are difficult, yet beneficial: working out, eating well, developing new skills, learning about intellectual subjects. These are all potentially difficult endeavors, yet also rewarding endeavors. This is the category of life processes that crying and other PMRs should be understood as belonging to.

Part of the discomfort around crying stems from the reality that crying is a vulnerable act. You are expressing and revealing to the world painful emotions, which *before they were released were being stored inside your own emotional-spiritual energies*. To cry is to admit to being in pain and having been in pain. It is also to demonstrate that you are moving on from the source of that pain.

We must begin to understand as a society that when a person cries, this is *only the release of someone's emotions*. Before being released, these emotions were part of the person, creating negative and potentially severe effects throughout their life, causing themselves and others to suffer. Above all else we should avoid anything that would cause us to hold on to negative emotional-spiritual energy longer than we need to.

When we adopt this new and often radical perspective, the experience of crying often changes dramatically and becomes much less difficult. It is like an experienced athlete who enjoys the challenging sensation of pushing themselves to the limit. For the Adoga practitioner, crying is merely a challenge, *where things get interesting*, not necessarily painful at all, no more "painful" than the sensation of running or lifting a heavy weight.

A Societal Shift Surrounding Emotional-Spiritual Expression

Laughing and sighing are more societally accepted than crying but are still often misunderstood. When you truly understand that laughing and sighing are manifestations of changing emotional-spiritual states, you'll begin to interpret the world quite differently.

All of these PMRs point to a broader truth and a broader change that society will need to embrace moving forward into the future. PMRs are one form of expressing our personal emotional-spiritual experience. On the whole, we need to become more welcoming and accepting of the expression of one's emotional-spiritual state. Pathology and underdevelopment are largely due to an inability for emotional-spiritual energy to flow between the internal self and the external world, as they naturally need and want to. If emotional-spiritual energies are trapped within you, unable to be released, they create problems on the inside which then are expressed as problems on the outside.

There is great motivation, however, to maintain the barriers that seal away emotional-spiritual energy within the self and prevent expression. Expressed emotional-spiritual states can affect others in harmful ways and, thus, it is necessary to create protective structures that make the expression of emotional-spiritual energy safe. Generally, self-growth practices that produce dramatic PMRs should be performed alone or with others who have a solid understanding of PMRs and their true meaning. If you are going to practice emotional-spiritual release with others, it is important to make sure that all people involved understand and consent to the activity that will take place. This forms a kind of context or container that allows for emotionally safe self-growth practice.

We can summarize the ethics present here as an acceptance of emotional-spiritual expression combined with a tempering and compassionate consideration for the effect such expression may have on others.

Physical Manifestations of Release (PMRs) in Adoga

PMRs should be expected in the practices of Adoga. If you are effective in creating changes to your emotional-spiritual state, then PMRs are only natural. Trying to stop your own process of release will only inhibit your progress. However, trying to force PMRs to happen will also be detrimental. Instead, you should focus on the intentions of the practices. From there simply allow the body to do what it wants to do naturally, and the PMRs will come as a result.

My experience points to the trend that less experienced practitioners may not experience PMRs intensely (or at all). With more experience, PMRs will come more readily and, as a result, your comfort with them will grow.

Other Physical Manifestations of Release (PMRs)

I see crying, laughing, and sighing as the primary PMRs, but there are others. Shaking is another possible PMR for example. Possible manifestations of creation-oriented shifts include: a change in posture, a relaxation of the muscles, a new facial expression or movement pattern. PMRs can take on lots of different forms. As you progress with your self-growth practice, see what physical experiences tend to accompany your emotional-spiritual changes.

Chapter Three
Oneness and the Ado

The DAO that can be expressed
is not the eternal DAO.

-Dao De Jing, An excerpt from Verse 1

If all on earth acknowledge the beautiful as beautiful
then thereby the ugly is already posited.
If all on earth acknowledge the good as good
then thereby is the non-good already posited.
For existence and non-existence generate each other.
Heavy and light complete each other.
Long and short shape each other.
High and deep convert each other.
Before and after follow each other.

-Dao De Jing, An excerpt from Verse 2

DAO generates the One.
The One generates the Two.
The Two generates the Three.
The Three generates all things.

-Dao De Jing, An excerpt from Verse 42

What Are Thoughts?

The practice of Adoga is a journey that takes us deep within ourselves. Its questions lead deep into life itself. To go further in understanding Adoga, we will need to create a philosophical foundation that can support the essential teachings and practice of this method.

The first question to address in creating this foundation is "What are thoughts?" or "What is thinking?" We humans are quite familiar with thinking. For many of us, it occupies our attention on a near constant basis. The ubiquity of thinking poses a challenge in forming a meaningful definition of thought. It is like the fish that swims in water all the time and thus has no idea it is swimming in water. The fish has never known anything else after all.

Fortunately, thinking is not completely constant. Some people report experiencing absences of thought. This is a common experience during meditation and times when we focus on present moment experience and sensory information rather than the analytical mind. Thoughts may also become quiet during moments of particular intensity, when we are called to respond with instinct.

We always experience thought on a spectrum from less active to more active. More thought activity produces the experience of an energetic or busy mind, even a hyper mind. Less thought activity produces the experience of a more open, peaceful, or still awareness. Being in a state of less thought activity does not necessarily mean that no thoughts arise in your awareness. Instead, it may mean that thoughts come less frequently or perhaps that thoughts are less fully formed, less fully articulated, eventually blending into a more felt quality of awareness. Both states of higher and lower mental activity have their purpose. I believe neither is necessarily better than the other. However, noticing the difference between greater and lesser thought activity helps to reveal, on an experiential level, the metaphorical water we are all swimming in.

This experiential understanding is useful as a reference point and as a context. However, to move forward, we will also need to define thinking in more exact terms:

I submit to you that thinking is the process we use to separate reality into things. A thing is a bit of reality that has a boundary. Bits of reality within the boundary are alike, while those outside the boundary represent some form of contrast. *Contrast* turns out to be central to this discussion. Notice that it is the lack of contrast that makes the water invisible to the fish. It is the presence of contrast that allows us to notice greater and lesser degrees of thought activity. Finally, it is contrast that will allow us to come to a solid, useful definition of thought. Thought is that which separates reality. In other words, thought is that which creates contrast.

Let's look at a couple examples. In defining any word or idea, we must use some form of contrast to create the definition. Left is the direction that is the opposite of right. Rectangles are shapes that have four sides but not three, not five, and not any other number. In every case, we must say a word or idea is defined by having certain characteristics while at the same time not having the opposing or contrasting characteristics. Definitions create a boundary around one patch of the universe where the given set of characteristics are present while outside of that patch those characteristics are not present. All definitions rely on these kinds of contrast-generating characteristics, and thinking, in turn, relies on definitions.

To say that something has a certain characteristic inherently implies the absence of an opposing characteristic. If a given direction *is* left, it is *not* right. If a given shape *is* a rectangle, it is *not* a triangle, a pentagon, or some other shape with more or less than four sides. By saying what something is, you also say, at the same moment, that there is a potential for it to be something else and that this potential has not been realized.

To think, to create a thought, is something like drawing a line on top of reality. A line that separates this from that, good from bad, joy from despair, left from right, rectangles from triangles, and triangles from pentagons, and so on. And we can draw our lines in different ways while continuing to accurately represent reality. For example, we can divide the concept of direction into two components – left and right – or we can take the same concept and divide it into 360 degrees. Both systems make sense and have the potential to accurately represent reality, but they draw different mental lines over the same patch of reality.

Note that it is only after an initial separation of reality into things or categories or objects that connections between these things, categories, or objects can be formed. It is only after the initial separations have been created by thought that things can form associations, relationships, and systems. After all, if you had no separated, defined things to start with, what could you possibly connect together or create a relationship between?

Thinking is thus first and most fundamentally an act of separating reality and only second an act of connecting it back together. Therefore, thinking is a central aspect of kav.

Oneness

What does reality look like prior to the separations, prior to thought? As mentioned before, some have reported the experience of an awareness that continues on without thinking. Such reports usually describe this non-mental awareness as being accompanied by a feeling of profound unity or *oneness*. When we look at our definition of thinking, this makes perfect sense. Without the separating process of thinking, reality feels un-separated – as if reality were only *one* thing. The term *non-dual* is another description of this state of awareness, which points to the same essential experience.

States of oneness can be created intentionally

through many practices. One simple and effective practice is the observation of the mind or the head center:

    To perform this practice, find a comfortable and relatively still position for your body. Then, watch your thinking as it occurs. Notice not just the thoughts themselves but also the quality of the thinking. Is your mind busy? Is your mind still? As you watch your thoughts and your level of mental activity, you will find yourself experiencing thoughts arising and falling away and then new thoughts arising and falling away. These cycles will happen naturally of their own accord. For this experiment, there is no need to attempt to influence your thinking directly in any particular way. We simply want to observe what is happening naturally. As the cycles occur, notice what your experience is like in the periods of falling away. You may find that there are pauses in between thoughts or even extended spaces. Through the simple observation of your mind and the absence of an intention to think, the mind will gradually become less active. Spaces will occur more frequently and for longer periods of time. Allow this calming of the mind to happen on its own. There is no need to force or even intend it directly.

    This practice will give you experiences outside of the mental realm, and thus outside of the dividing and separating mechanism of thought. Traveling out of our typical mentally focused awareness reveals to our metaphorical fish-selves that water is only one of many possible environments. There are whole other modes of being, different contexts in which life can unfold. There are several potential benefits to doing this exercise, but for this discussion we can use this meditation, especially, as a way of understanding oneness, non-duality, and yune as meaningful experiences rather than only as abstract concepts.

Integrating all of this into our philosophical foundation, we can articulate the following summary: First, there is a unified, unseparated reality. Then, thinking separates reality into distinct and contrasted things or categories. And finally, thinking can create connections, associations, and systems of various degrees of complexity out of the distinct and contrasted things or categories.

Form, Holan, and Energy

Let's turn our attention to the things or categories that emerge from the separating process of thought. I think it is amusing and insightful to notice the profundity of the word *thing*. A thing describes an object separated from the rest of reality – a patch of reality with a boundary around it. In this section, we will explore several terms that mean something close to the word *thing*, though each will define their own distinctive variation or flavor of this central idea.

We can define a *form* as an object that possesses characteristics, distinct from other possibilities in the universe. I like the term *form* because it brings to mind the shape or boundary of something, which I think is a good analogy to the various ways that things can possess characteristics. In contrast, *formlessness* refers to the possibility of being without characteristics or, at least, being without clear definition.

Next, let us consider the terms *holan* and *holarchy*, originally introduced by Arthur Koestler in his 1967 book *The Ghost in the Machine*. A holan is something that functions as both a part and a whole. A holarchy, referencing the concept of a hierarchy, is a collection or system of holans that is structured into levels such that some holans combine to form larger and more encompassing holans that in turn combine to form still larger and more encompassing holans, and so on. Each holan then functions as a whole in the context of the smaller and less encompassing holans it comprises while also functioning as a part in the context of a larger and more encompassing holan.

A good example of a holarchy might be the taxonomy used in the study of biology where life is categorized into domains that are further categorized into kingdoms, which are then further categorized into phyla, and so on. Indeed, the words *taxonomy* and *hierarchy* can mean something similar to *holarchy*. However, I am fond of using the terms *holan* and *holarchy* as a pair because this method provides a useful term to describe the items in the holarchy – the holans – while also nicely describing the whole and part nature of the structure.

I also like using the term *tree* to refer to holarchies because it brings to mind a visual representation of these kinds of structures where holans break off into several parts that continue to break off into more and more parts like the branches of a tree.

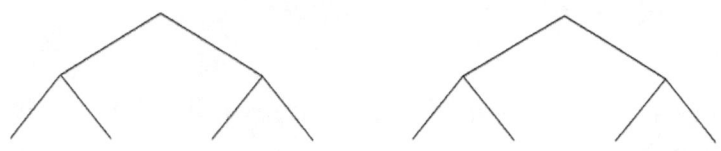

Finally, let's consider that all forms and holans are imbued with *energy* – an idea that we have already touched on in Chapter One. In physics, energy refers to the capacity to do work. The word *energy* comes from the Greek *energeia* – combining *en* meaning in or within and *ergon*, which means work. So the meaning of the word might be translated as the work within something. In the contexts of self-growth and spirituality, energy takes on a more metaphorical and nonphysical meaning, but the essential idea of the capacity for work remains the same. Energy is the functional aspect of a form; it refers to what a form does or has the potential to do.

    I also use the word *energy* to refer to the more felt, intuitive, or present moment aspect of an experience. In contrast, I use *form* to highlight the aspect of experience that has definition and *holan* to highlight connection to a broader system of hierarchy (or holarchy in our new vernacular).

    Form, holan, and energy each refer an essential aspect of all things. All things have definition (form), connection to the broader system (holarchy), and functional potential (energy).

The Principle of Infinite Potential

Is there a biggest holan? Does the tree of division continue infinitely?

We have posited that we could define thinking as a process of generating contrast and that all definitions rely on contrast. This is what creates the boundary of a form. In order for a form or holan to exist meaningfully, it must have certain characteristics while not having the opposing or contrasting characteristics. What provides an ultimately biggest or ultimately encompassing or ultimately inclusive form with contrast? If it is ultimately inclusive where will we find opposing characteristics to create this necessary contrast? How can we possibly define such a form? I don't think we really can. Even defining it as all-inclusive seems to be paradoxical. If it is all-inclusive does it include as a part of its own characteristics that it is exclusive, partial, or incomplete? If it does not include those things, does it count as all-inclusive?

Let's look at the situation with an analogy. Let's imagine that we have a form that is represented by the shape of a circle. The circle creates a boundary. It creates contrast, so that reality outside the circle is not part of the holan, whereas reality inside the circle is part of the holan. So far, so good.

Now, let's say that if the circle expands it includes

Chapter Three • Oneness and the Ado

more of reality, becoming more encompassing and becoming a larger holan. If the circle were to expand infinitely, creating the biggest possible holan, we run into the problem that nothing exists outside of the circle to give it shape. There is no contrast, thus no definition. It is no longer a circle. We need to set the circle in a context that is large enough to reveal what happens on the outside of the circle for us to be able to see the shape.

Any way you look at it, I think we must conclude that the mysterious all-inclusive holan eludes definition and all forms of sense-making. However, the all-inclusive holan is the very same idea as oneness or non-duality, which are actually better terms because the all-inclusive holan turns out to not be a holan. Holans are simultaneously parts and wholes. Something that is all-inclusive does not function as a part. Holans also have definitions and contrast. Oneness does not. For me, this transition from defined holans to undefined, mysterious oneness is the meeting of philosophy and spirituality, of rational thought and something beyond logic.

Though we may not be able to define oneness completely or perhaps even at all, many report experiencing a sense of oneness. By following the exercise of observing your mind we discussed earlier, you can experience this for yourself as well. To be truly accurate though, we have to acknowledge that personal experiences also create partialness and separation, just as thinking does. Consider, for example, that personal experience must include only your experience but not the experience of others. Consider, also, that personal experiences or events occur at certain points in time and not others. Therefore, anything particular to your experience or a certain point in time will still fall short of true oneness. However, in the absence of thought we do experience a *sense of oneness* as our awareness moves into its most unified potential states.

So then, the truest conception of oneness is not an idea, not an experience, but simply... life, everything, all that is and was and will be, the good and the bad, your experiences and the experiences of others, sentience and the lack thereof, consciousness and unconsciousness.

The ancient spiritual book known as the Dao De Jing describes pure and absolute oneness as Dao. Its opening line encapsulates much of the wisdom that we are uncovering: "The DAO that can be expressed is not the eternal DAO." Although we can point toward oneness with various descriptions, any characterization or expression represents a selection within and thus limitation of all possibilities. Therefore, anything we say about oneness will not be able to encapsulate the fullness of this reality, which is the fullness of all reality.

Our philosophical foundation then seems to comprise two fundamental pieces: 1) Oneness, which exists independent of thought and eludes definition, and 2) Holarchy, which is created by thought and possesses definition.

If true oneness cannot be defined, it seems to follow that, for the same reasons, it cannot be fully known, explored, or manifested. This insight seems to point to an exciting aspect of our reality: We live in a world where discovery and development are infinitely unfolding processes in a container without boundary, without limit, and without ending. I like to think of this realization as the principle of infinite potential.

This is not to say that the universe in its current, physical form is infinite. It is only to say that the possibilities of evolution are boundless. Boundaries create limitations in numerous ways and yet numerous opportunities for novelty and expansion also seem to continuously present themselves to the attentive mind. Thus, although we can characterize aspects of life's evolutionary unfolding, its totality remains mysterious.

If you feel unconvinced about the principle of infinite potential at this point, that's fine. And if that is the case, you might consider that philosophical debates aside, from a practical point of view the amount of potential skill development, exploration, and growth in this universe is, at least, truly immense. If these things are not infinite in a literal and abstract way, they may be practically infinite or, in other words, so vast that our personal experience need not be concerned with their limitations.

The principle of infinite potential in literal or practical interpretations does set a game-changing context for the world of self-growth. The implication is that there is always room to grow. We never reach a state of perfection but instead are tasked with the pursuit of continually higher developmental capacities. It means that there is no final destination that we can permanently hold on to.

Instead, there are periodic destinations along the journey, as we master one context and move on to another.

The principle of infinite potential applies to the dividing and summing processes of the mental realm and also to emotional and spiritual development. Note that mental, emotional, and spiritual developmental all produce a diversified, contrast-generating set of experiences, which generally becomes structured into holarchies over time. Although emotional and spiritual holarchies do not possess the sharp and clear definitions of thinking, they still possess contrast in a softer, less exact way. Emotional and spiritual experiences create unique kinds of flavors and characteristics. Some experiences have many parts or aspects, creating levels of holarchy.

Let's consider the analogy of creating an ever-expanding map of reality. Over time, we continuously improve our maps more and more, making them more and more accurate, but they never quite become the same as the actual territory they describe. Nor do we ever run out of new territory to discover and map. Our intellectual holarchies are like the maps we use to describe reality. Emotionally and spiritually, we experience an ever-expanding perception of the territory our maps attempt to describe through a different lens.

The image on the next page represents one possible depiction of such a map, arranged in a holarchy.

Chapter Three • Oneness and the Ado

The mind creates maps of the world by breaking things apart and relating them in structures like the ones shown in this image. The borders of the map fade representing the way in which knowledge blends into mystery.

The World of the Ado

We are now poised to move away from general self-growth foundations and into the world of Adoga, which begins with the *ado*. Ado is an acronym that stands for *archetypal division of oneness*. An ado is essentially a big-picture or generally applicable pattern or archetype – but not just any big-picture pattern, specifically a pattern that attempts to capture the biggest picture possible. Adoga is extended version of this acronym – *archetypal divisions of oneness growth activity* – and refers to the self-growth practice that is based on the theory of ados.

An archetype in this context simply refers to a big-picture pattern. Division of oneness refers to a central question and premise for our study: "Where does thinking begin?" If we make only a single division to an otherwise unified reality – to oneness – and thereby create two parts, the most basic of holarchies, what do these parts look like? And continuing this train of thought, what if we were to create three fundamental parts or four or five? What would these look like? What if we created subdivisions of the parts?

What these look like, to begin with, are ados. These are the divisions of oneness or the parts of oneness that are

Chapter Three • Oneness and the Ado

the most general, the most encompassing. What I have described as yune and kav are the most fundamental of ados – a vision of reality separated only once into two, highly encompassing parts.

I can imagine an important objection being raised at this point: If we can't define oneness, how could we possibly define half of it? And if we could define two halves of oneness, could we not simply put these together to produce a definition of the elusive and infinite oneness? Claiming that a defined ado represents a percentage of infinity would be problematic, but ados actually break apart what we could think of as *known oneness* – the summation of what is known. Known oneness is a holan. It can be defined. It has contrast by virtue of being different than the unknown and the partially known.

Although known oneness is a holan, its unique position within the holarchy of human knowledge and experience does present a certain challenge in defining it. If we were to create a definition of known oneness, we could also easily imagine the opposite of our definition. And as soon as we do so, we are left with more characteristics to include into our definition. For example, if we say that the defining characteristic of known oneness is beauty, we could then ask why we did not include ugliness. If we say the defining characteristic is change, we could inquire about stasis.

The way to overcome this challenge, I think, is with ados. If we define known oneness, not with a single characteristic but with a balanced set of characteristics, we can produce a stable definition. And our study of ados moving forward will begin to paint exactly this kind of picture of known oneness.

New Words

You may have noticed that as we go along we are creating and introducing more and more new words – yune, kav, oneness, holan, holarchy, ado, form, and so on. There is a good reason for this.

In the various self-growth communities, a problem commonly arises where new perceptions and experiences are made available by the self-growth work and precisely because the perceptions and experiences are new either to the individual or the community at large, there seems to be no good words to describe them.

Now this by itself is not too much of a problem, but there is a common misperception that spiritual ideas are always difficult to express. This leads many self-growthers to assume that their difficulty in expressing their experiences is inevitable and to be expected. When in reality, we simply need to name our experiences and take measures to ensure a collective understanding of that naming.

It is often claimed that words could not capture this or that experience. And that may be a fine way to describe the situation, but people often do not realize that words always fail to capture the experience they represent. The word *chair*, for example, is not that same as the actual chair it is referencing. And because of this gap between language and reality, certain limitations arise. Upon hearing "chair" (and nothing else), I cannot say what it feels like or what kind of material it is made out of or how big it is. Though if I were right in front of a chair, having the experience myself, I certainly could.

So words fall short of the experience, to a degree. However, naming these objects that we sit on still seems like a useful and reasonable idea. In fact, it would seem incredibly inconvenient not to do this. After all, while not capturing the entirety of the experience, the word *chair* still conveys a lot of good information – that we are talking about a physical object, what its purpose and general shape is, and so on.

These points all apply equally to words that refer to experiences in the realms of spirituality and self-growth. The difference is that, while most people have experienced chairs, people's experiences in spirituality and self-growth vary more widely. And this means that if I'm trying to convey an experience to you that you have never encountered, nor even anything remotely similar, then I can come up with all the words I want and no real communication will occur.

However, between two people who have both had a similar set of experiences, words serve as a simple indicator for and representation of something we both understand. The word, by itself, does not give us the understanding, but it is useful for communication once the initial understanding has already been achieved.

With this perspective in mind, I generally argue in favor of naming things that need names. Of course, we only need so many words. At a certain point, new words might become redundant. But I feel strongly in support of creating new words for experiences that truly cannot be described well and in modifying our vocabularies to be able to describe things better and better, with more clarity, ease, and depth of understanding.

In essence, what we are talking about here is the creation of a new language, and, in fact, this has been going on since the beginning of language itself. Language has evolved and will evolve whether we want it to or not. However, we can choose to consciously participate in that evolution or we can choose to sit on the sidelines.

I feel that this is an important topic because the way we use language affects both how we think and how we relate. By upgrading our language, we upgrade our thinking and relating too.

Tree Language

This leads us into our last section for this chapter in which we will discuss what I call *tree language*. Tree language is a method of describing holans and holarchies mathematically, especially within the context of ado structures. Tree language uses a series of numbers separated by periods to describe the position and definition of a holan in a tree. Look at the diagram on the following page to see an example of a tree labeled with tree language.

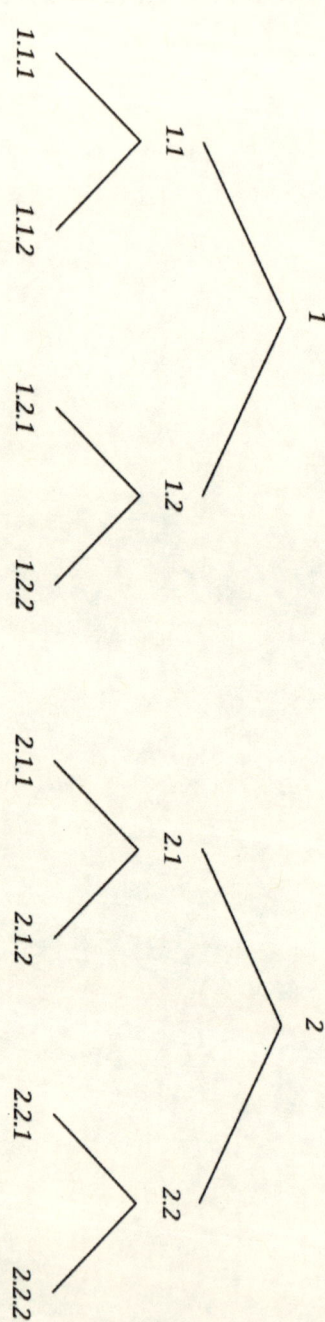

Notice that this tree has three levels of division: the two-part level of division, the four-part level of division, and the eight-part level of division. Tree language designations describe the pathway used to arrive at a given holan traveling down the tree from more general to more specific levels of division. Numbers describe the choice made at a particular choice-point where a holan divides into more specific parts. Periods indicate that the following number will describe the next most specific level of division in the tree. For example, 1.2 describes a holan that is defined by the first part of the most general level of division, and, within that, the second part of the next most specific level of division. In the case of the tree above, this would be the holan that is contained within the left half of the two-part division and occupies the second quarter of the four-part division.

In this book, we will use only the levels of division and the accompanying tree language shown in the diagram on the previous page. However, a level of division could contain any number of parts. Notice that in our current tree language there is no way to differentiate between the second choice of two parts or the second choice of three parts, just to mention one possible example. An extra step can be included in tree language that allows us to describe the holans that exist on any level of division. We can indicate the number of possible choices at a given choice-point by using a slash followed by the number of possibilities. For example, 1/3 describes the first choice out of three possibilities and can be read as "one of three." The

1.2 holan we mentioned previously in our tree diagram can also be described as 1/2.2/2. This indicates that the holan is contained within the first of two parts and occupies the second of two parts within the first designation.

We can continue to add numbers and periods indefinitely to a tree language designation to describe any position on any potential tree. When referencing an established tree where the levels of division are already known, we can make our tree language shorter by excluding slashes and their following numbers. In this book, we will be discussing only binary divisions and nested binary divisions (meaning binary divisions within binary divisions). So for the sake of brevity, we will say that a "/2" is implied in all our tree language designations moving forward.

Tree language is useful for describing ados because it is free of characteristics or associations beyond the fundamental mathematical structure involved. For example, 1 (or 1/2) as an ado describes the most fundamental definition of this concept: the first of two parts when known oneness is divided in two. From this point, we can go into studying more elaborate definitions and descriptions of each of these ados, even evolving these definitions and descriptions over time, while still referring to consistent positions within the ado tree.

Each position within the ado tree also has a separate name that has been designed to sound like the meaning of that particular ado. These names are also relatively free of associations; however, they provide an intuitive feel for each place in the tree. These names are listed in the diagram on the following page. Throughout the next four chapters, we will explore the meaning of all of these ados.

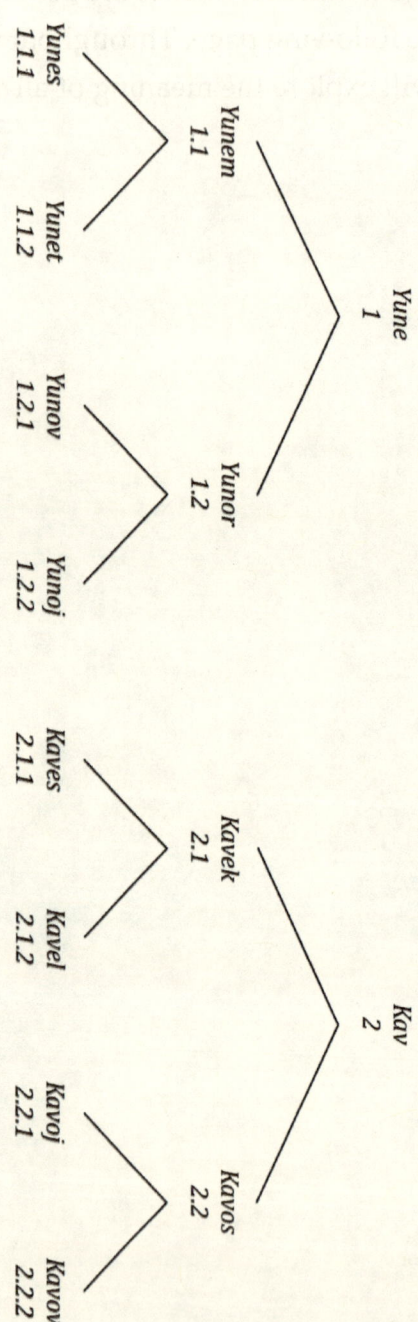

Part II

The Four Trees of Adoga

Chapter Four
The Tree of Practices

With a philosophical and practical foundation in place, we can now progress into discussing the *four trees of Adoga*. These trees are holarchies that outline what we do in the Adoga practice as well as the experiences that may arise in Adoga and in life generally. We can also think of these trees as *maps* that describe the *territory* of four different contexts. In this chapter, we will begin with the tree of practices, which describes what we *do* in Adoga.

Adoga is like a *meta*-practice in that it contains many interrelated practices. Theoretically, there is a practice associated with every possible position of the holarchy – an endless list, in fact. In this chapter, we will cover six of the most primary practices. In tree language, these are the practices associated with 1, 2, 1.1, 1.2, 2.1, and 2.2.

On the following page, you'll find a visual illustration of these practices. I've included the name of each ado position, the associated tree language, and brief descriptor of the practice associated with each ado.

Chapter Four • The Tree of Practices

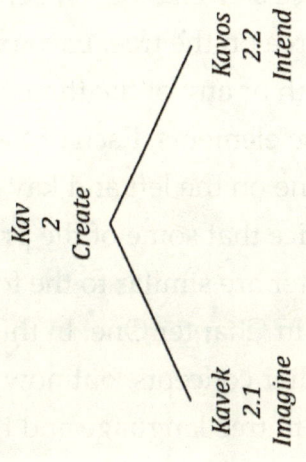

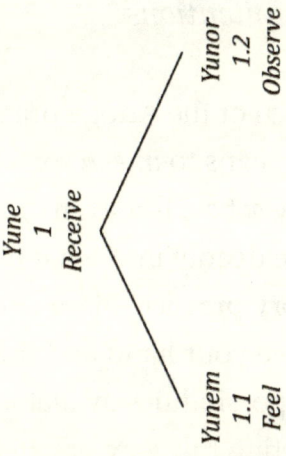

In the following sections, I'll describe each practice on this diagram one at a time. We will discuss both how to perform each practice as well as a few self-growth concepts that relate to each area on the tree. Each practice can be focused on the breath or any of the three centers or any combination of these elements. Each of the four trees forms a spectrum with yune on the left and kav on the right.

You may notice that some of the practices we discuss in this chapter are similar to the foundational practices discussed in Chapter One. In this chapter, we will consider some familiar concepts, but now in more depth and also in relation to tree language and the Adoga framework. After becoming acquainted with each of the practices on the tree individually, we will eventually move on to combining them all together into an integrated, broad-spectrum framework.

An Introduction to Intentions

Before discussing each of the Adoga practices, we must understand what it means to *intend* something. Every *practice*, indeed every *action*, is a form of *intention*.

To delve more deeply into what it means to *intend*, let's try an exploratory practice. Place one of your hands in front of you and move your hand and fingers in different ways, exploring the possibilities available in the motion of your hand… contracting this way or extending that way… Notice while you do this what or who is making the hand move. Where is the self that intends the hand to move?

Notice the feeling of *intention*, as it connects the internal realm of the self to the external realm of manifestation where your hand follows the intended directions.

One of the most essential parts of being alive is our ability to intend, our existence as creators. You wield the power of intention. It is an energy that flows from your consciousness out into the manifested world. I invite you to experience these truths as you practice using your intention in this simple way.

Now, let us consider that intentions do not have to be physical. Intention can act within the emotional, mental, and spiritual realms as well, and it functions in much the same way. It merely acts upon something different. In the following sections, we will explore ways we can use our intention in the emotional-spiritual realm.

As we go through each practice, I'll do my best to describe *how* to perform each intention powerfully. We don't want to overthink how to perform these intentions. Sometimes the method of performing an intention is simpler than it seems. We might need only to get in touch with our intention and persistently direct it to where we want to go. Other times, we may find it useful to explore the subtleties of performing an intention, diving deeply into what we can do with our intention and how it works.

Receive (Yune 1)

Yune, as a practice, is the intention of receiving. Yune entails noticing your experience in the present moment. It means noticing your physical sensations, emotions, thoughts, and intuitions. It means noticing everything and anything that comes up. I invite you to try this out as you read these words.

Primarily, the yune practice is not selective. You do not choose what you want to receive or notice. Instead, you see what in your experience seems to *want to be received*. You let your experience talk to you and you do your best to *listen*. If you relax your intention, you may notice that you are pulled to focus on certain aspects of your experience. The invitation in this practice is to follow this pull and *take in* all that can be experienced through the journey. In this way, yune is open to the great generality of experience rather than being focused or directed toward specific forms in the multiplicity of life's possibilities.

By receiving your experience, you will learn so much about yourself and life in general. You may discover emotions that you did not know existed within you. This practice can also lead to the spontaneous discovery of ideas, awareness, and inspirations.

One way of performing the yune receiving practice is to ask yourself, "How are you doing?" and then listen to the answer, as it is reported by your feelings and experience, continuously, deeply, and very curiously.

Though receiving is an intention, much of the practice actually entails relaxing intentions. As you notice and take in the experiences that come up, you will probably find *resistances* to those experiences – meaning an unconscious use of our intention power that keeps certain things out of our awareness and domain of feeling. Resistances *repress* our feelings and experience creating a situation where we either do not know that certain aspects of our experience exist at all or we may have a limited or distorted awareness of our true emotional-spiritual condition. Relaxing resistances is a challenge. They are there to protect us from painful feelings. But relaxing resistances is exactly what we must do in order to heal our repressions and grow our awareness.

When painful experiences come into awareness asking to be received, we must keep in mind that it is *okay* to be uncomfortable, even in pain. Often, the best path forward involves pain. Though we don't like pain, it is a necessary part of life. And without it, life would be less than whole. It plays a part in growth, in the appreciation of good things, and in the creation of a deeply meaningful world, where experiences are rich, colorful, and diverse rather than monochromatic, static, and dull.

Carrying this perspective can allow you to be more accepting of discomfort and pain, which in the end will make you more comfortable and more happy. I like to use the analogy of training for physical fitness. Lifting weights may be uncomfortable and hard, but it is also rewarding. Successful athletes grow to enjoy challenging themselves, enduring discomfort so that they can achieve something fulfilling and exciting. Self-growth is exactly the same way. We must learn to interpret discomfort as an enjoyable and rewarding challenge.

In physical fitness training, there are two types of

discomfort: the type that means you are challenging yourself and the type that means you are injuring yourself. The same goes for self-growth. You should feel challenging discomfort, as if lifting a challenging weight. If you start to feel as though you are being *injured*, stop, recover, and come back to your practice when you are ready, perhaps with appropriate modifications.

When we intend to receive or take in our experience, our repressed pain naturally comes to the surface. It takes courage to face that pain. Receiving requires the courage to be vulnerable and honest with yourself. You don't have to *like* the repressed experiences that emerge in order to receive them. You don't have believe the thoughts that emerge or think that the emotions that emerge are beneficial. You need only to become aware of them, completely and compassionately.

At times, the receiving practice may need us to be *very gentle*. The yune area of consciousness is not a world where forcing things works well. In the yune practice, we have a formed and clear intention to listen to our experience, but it is a gentle intention. It intently seeks to follow, learn about, and discover your own experience. It does not demand that certain outcomes are achieved nor that our experience responds in a specific way.

It is like gently asking a close friend to share something personal. In yune receiving, we develop the capacity for a kind of loving care and quality listening that is *directed toward yourself*. When we can care for ourselves in this way, we can care for others more effectively too.

Create (Kav 2)

In the kav practice, we create desired emotional-spiritual energy and a desired emotional-spiritual state. In Adoga, the goal is always, in one way or another, to improve one's state. However, in kav creating we directly intend the state we desire. Unlike yune receiving, where we set our intention on following our experience, here our intention must take the lead, directly acting on and influencing our experience in the ways we desire. As a result of creating a new and improved emotional-spiritual state, we will find that new ideas, perspectives, physical conditions, and external life circumstances will be created or affected positively.

As we will discover in more depth later on, a big part of creating a new state is being able to *imagine* the given state with *clarity*, so that your intention to create will be focused on a *specific* reality. We have to know what reality we want to create before we can create it.

Kav is about the exploration of a vast and diverse array of emotional-spiritual states. Here, oneness breaks apart into the *divine many* – a multiplicity of states – from which we must choose what to explore, focus on, and create.

Often when you set your intention to create a particular state, rather than experiencing the intended state, you will experience all your resistances to being in the intended state instead. If this happens, there is no need to worry. In fact, rejoice. You have now brought the barriers to your success into the light of your awareness where they can be addressed.

In this situation, one possibility is to switch over to the yune receiving practice upon experiencing the resistances that arise in your emotional-spiritual state. This is often the best choice for strong resistances. Yune receiving will help to alleviate resistances and, after practicing receiving for a period of time, you may find that you can complete the goal of forming the intended state with the kav creating practice. Weaker resistances can sometimes be addressed by simply continuing the kav intending practice with persistence.

We will discuss how to perform the yune receiving and kav creating practices in more detail later in this chapter. For now, we'll move on to the practices associated with the four-part division on our tree – feel (yunem 1.1), observe (yunor 1.2), imagine (kavek 2.1), and intend (kavos 2.2).

The Method of Discovering Ados

We are going to begin this examination of practices on the four-part level of division with the 1.2 observing practice. There is an important reason for starting in this position. It is often easiest to understand the kav components of a yune holan before learning about the yune components of a yune holan. Similarly, it is easiest to understand the yune components of a kav holan before understanding the kav components of a kav holan.

The guiding principle here is this: Holans that create contrast in comparison to their larger, more encompassing, "parent" holans, if you will, provide a clear starting point for new definitions. Holans that lack this kind of contrast – for example yune components of yune holans – are often best understood in the context of already established holans which *do* create contrast.

Once we establish a basic understanding of a few ado positions in this chapter. We will be able to use our established understanding as a reference point and will, generally, add new layers of understanding from yune to kav or perhaps in some contexts from kav to yune. After introducing all the practices we will cover in this chapter, we will review the material we have just learned in order from yune to kav to help solidify and integrate the new knowledge.

Observe (Yunor 1.2)

Yunor practice is, to begin with, a form of yune receiving but with some kind of a kav flavor thrown into the mix. In most cases, this kav flavor takes the form of a *focus* that creates a higher intensity of expressive intention and a greater degree of specificity. A classic form of the yunor practice is to set the intention of observing your breath, gently bring your attention back to breathing whenever you become distracted. (Keep in mind that you can create variations of this practice by changing the object of your focus to one of the three energetic centers – gut, heart, or head – or any other center of subtle energy you are in contact with.)

Try the practice of observing your breathing now. The difficulty of this practice is largely in its simplicity. We want to observe, just observe, nothing else. There is no need to intend any changes to your state, simply observe. If other experiences arise alongside your breath in your field of awareness, that is fine. You can allow yourself to take these in as well, always staying centered on the experience of breathing.

As you watch your breath, you may become increasingly aware of the part of the self that observes – the *observing self*. As this awareness grows, the practice can become more about being aware of the observing self than observing the breath. The observing self is an open, spacious experience. It is unattached – unattached to outcomes, to particular types of experiences, to directions toward good things, or away from bad things. It simply is. It simply watches. When experiences of attachments, preferences, or wants arise, these can be observed just as all experience can be. And, just as with all experiences, the observing self will be unattached, even to the experience of attachment.

The observing self is a yune part of yourself. It is connected to oneness, undivided, and thus without direction, without desire or focused intention. Feelings of being connected with, even one with, or *the same as* the world around you may arise as your awareness of the observing self grows.

You may notice a certain kind of division along with the sense of oneness: the division between the observing self and the observed experience. This division is part of what comes with the kav flavor that is added to the more general yune receiving and taking in practice. If this division is eliminated, the practice transforms into yunem (1.1), which we will discuss in the next section. Both divided and undivided receiving have advantages.

A separated observing self creates *freedom* from one's experience. Without it, we are bound to, invested in, and attached to our experience in ways that can be rigid and unhelpful. I like to think that freedom, in various forms, is one of the primary virtues of yunor. It allows us to see things in ways that transcend our old perspectives and habits. It allows us to eliminate false or limiting assumptions about ourselves and the world. It allows us to break out of limiting beliefs of all kinds, to be *free* of them and embrace greater levels of potential. All of these benefits require a certain quality of separation from one's emotions and observed experience in general. In yunor practice, we are tasked with developing a sense of perspective on our experience.

The division between observer and observed in yunor is also the source of the observing self, which gifts us with expansive consciousness and a connection to oneness and the divine. This awareness provides a deep sense of connection and a profound understanding of how things fit into the big-picture of life. The expansiveness of its view allows us to see the perfection in every little thing.

Feel (Yunem 1.1)

If the yunor (1.2) observing practice is a form of yune (1) receiving with a focusing aspect and a division between the observer and the observed, yunem (1.1) feeling is a form of yune (1.1) receiving without focus or division between the observer and the observed. In the world of yunem, there is no observer. There is only experience... experience and the happening of experience.

The term *opening* is a good descriptor of the yunem feeling practice. It means opening yourself up to your feelings and your experience. It means to be vulnerable with yourself. We can imagine that there is an endless stream of experiences and emotions asking to come into awareness and flow through you. The yunem practice is the activity of saying yes to experiencing these feelings and awarenesses one after another, in flowing waves of reception.

Rather than a sense of freedom and expansiveness like yunor, yunem provides a sense of depth and aliveness. As experiences course through you, raw energy and awareness is released into your being as potential. To succeed in creating the benefits of this practice, you must commit to being with and being one with your experience and your feelings, without filter, without holding back. You must allow the fullness and richness of your experience to come through.

Like yune practice in general, this requires courage but also gentleness. Emotions will not come if you try to force them to the surface. Instead, the effective yunem *feeler* will make a space where the depth and vulnerability of emotions are accepted and appreciated. Then, it is a matter of *allowing* – a gentle intention – the experiences that are asking to arise to reveal themselves in their fullest nature.

The experience of yunem can be difficult at times, though it can also be immensely rewarding, invigorating, and enlivening. You feel as though the act of releasing pent-up, repressed experiences opens up a space, where fresh, raw consciousness and energy comes in and permeates your being.

To get a practical taste of yunem, you might try starting by focusing on your heart and the emotions and feelings that live around that area in your body. If you have a strong intuition of what experience is asking to flow through you next, you may not need this focus on the heart center; rather, you can simply follow your intuition's guidance. But if you are searching for a starting place, the heart is a good one.

Now, allow and gently invite your experience to arise fully in your awareness. Relax. Intend to feel more of your experience again and again, relaxing more deeply each time. This is the practice of *experiencing more* by *relaxing more*. Keep yourself just focused and awake enough to *be present* for the experiences that will arise but no more. If you notice any inclinations to *turn away* or *resist* the arising experiences, to the best of your ability, *relax* and remind yourself that you are committed to experiencing the truth of how you feel, your true condition and experience. Become intensely curious about this truth. Let your curiosity, your acceptance, your "okay-ness" with emotion and vulnerability guide you into a deeper, more truthful, and more alive awareness and perception.

In yunor (1.2) observing there is a sense of distance between "you" or the observer and your experience. In yunem (1.1) feeling, we want to collapse that distance. One thing I find helpful here is to not think too much. Thinking creates division and contrast. In yunem, we seek unity.

When there is no distance between you and your emotions, you'll feel like you are experiencing your emotions fully. They can seem to take you over. You become them and they become you. You become emotional but intentionally and consciously so.

Imagine (Kavek 2.1)

Now we will jump over to the kav (2) half of the tree, starting with the kavek (2.1) imagining practice. We can think of kavek practice as a form of kav (2) creation with a tempering yune aspect to it. We can see this yune aspect as the *potential* embedded within imagination. The imagination is the space within ourselves where we create potential realities, visions that may become manifestations in the external world through repeated focus and action.

Though we want to manifest our desires into their final forms where we can benefit from them, potentials have advantages and purpose, in and of themselves. You don't have to commit to potentials and imaginations like you do for manifestations. Imagining being a successful entrepreneur can be accomplished quickly.

Being a successful entrepreneur, however, is a much longer journey. To *manifest* this reality takes years of hard work. Of course, you don't get the benefits of the manifestation from the imagination alone, but the imagination does allow you to test out a multitude of possibilities and variations with relatively little investment of time or energy.

Imagination is a superb way to discover what you like and dislike, what you think is important and not important, where you want to go and what you find exciting. It is also a testing ground where we discover a lot about what might work well or not work well in the real world. And that's another benefit of imagination – failures don't cost you much. This means that imagining what we *don't want* is just as valuable as imagining what we *do want*.

In kavek, the objective is not directly creating an improved emotional-spiritual state. Instead, the objective is to expand our knowledge and awareness of what I like to call the *possibility space* – in other words, the set of all possibilities within a certain context. For example, kavek imagination with regard to your career could help you to be aware of all the possible career paths, subjects, and styles of contribution that exist as potentials in the working world. What is most important for this area of life? Is it having a purpose that you are passionate about? What does life look like with and without this quality? What about the relationships associated with your work? What do good relationships look like to you and what do bad ones look like? In any endeavor, there is so much to explore, and in the end, imagination practice provides both a lot of information and a direction that is inspiring to pursue.

Kavek is fun and exciting. You get to play "make your own life" and without the costs of effort and challenge that accompany manifested endeavors. It is not a requirement for imagination to be realistic either. You can play with this factor, trying out more presumably realistic options and less realistic ones. Sometimes, it can be fun and even useful to throw realism out completely. What if magic were allowed? What if we lived in a fantastical land or a far-future sci-fi landscape? What about another life back in time, in some fascinating nook of history? Or... maybe in this world you cannot speak... perhaps there are multiple universes that interact with each other... maybe you have a pet hippopotamus or your consciousness controls three separate bodies...

Imagination can be funny. It can be weird. It can be a lot of different things and that is part of the fun. It can be ridiculous. And sometimes ridiculousness can be useful. Kavek seeks to explore, know, and learn about more and more of the world's possibility space. Understanding a greater amount of the possibility space is the direction of improvement in this practice. Therefore, we will want to consider as many things as possible. We will want to think through things that sound ridiculous to make sure we aren't overlooking any limitations around those strange, bizarre, and ridiculous areas.

In addition, the limitations of the possibility space we have access to are often there because a resistance or emotional-spiritual barrier prevents our consciousness from reaching certain areas of potentiality. By challenging the edges of the possibility space we have access to, we can see what our limits are and what resistances might be behind those limits. When limitations are exposed, they can be resolved and transformed simply by becoming aware of them or, if a given resistance is strong, they may be addressed with a yune practice: yune (1) receiving, yunem (1.1) feeling, or yunor (1.2) observing. By becoming *aware* of limitations we gain an important advantage in overcoming them.

There are four important variations of kavek practice that we can explore:

1. Imagine something simple.

2. Imagine something totally different than your current experience.

3. Imagine something you want.

4. Imagine something you do not want.

Option one on this list is what I call *simple imagination practice*. Simple imagination practice is useful in a few ways. To begin with, sometimes our imagination does things we aren't aware of – things that we may have never consciously intended to do. And sometimes these subconscious or unintentional imaginative processes are generating emotions or states that are detrimental to our well-being. If this is the case, any imaginative practice will help, but simple imagination is optimal. The reason being that, before introducing any more complexity, we need our imagination to stop what it is doing and return its energy to a clean form of potential that we can use for something more constructive. The best way to accomplish this is to direct the imagination toward conscious simplicity. From this foundation, we can build up to complex imaginations more effectively.

One of my favorite simple imaginations is a black circle or dot on a white background. Sometimes I'll add a black rectangular border around the circle and have the circle move slowly, bouncing off the border should it ever reach it. Variations of this can be created by using different shapes, colors, and sizes. Another idea is peaceful natural environments, beaches, forests, whatever you find relaxing and nonthreatening. You can also see what happens if you intend to imagine a vast space or void, perhaps colored black or white.

It can be amazing how difficult imagining the simple things can be. Sometimes it can feel more difficult than imagining more complicated things. Though they might not sound exciting on the surface, these exercises are very valuable for developing the ability to imagine what you want and to do so consciously. Like the practice of observing your breathing, simple imagination exercise can be a wonderful tool for developing a greater capacity for *focus* and this translates into many areas of life. You can challenge your focus by continuing to imagine a single, simple imagination for an extended period of time.

As you practice simple imagination, you may notice that sometimes your imaginations don't obey your instructions, as if they have a mind of their own. Be patient with this, but do not follow your imagination's whim. This is a kav practice overall, which means that we must use our intention to take the lead, rather than following our experience. If your imagination wanders from your intention, keep intending with persistence. Try to create a state where you are in control of your imaginative space.

We said that simple imagination was one of four options we can explore in kavek practice. In options two, three, and four, we will emphasize creating variations of imagined experiences. We want to explore what is possible, push the limits, and also curiously check out the diversity. Not everything needs to be extreme, that too would be limiting. Then again, not everything needs to be moderate either. The idea is to expand your awareness. Whatever direction looks like an uncharted potential for expansion – that's the direction you want to go in.

As you do this, stay in touch with your emotional-spiritual state. See how you respond to the different possibilities. When resistances arise – as they surely will if you are pushing the limitations of your personal possibility space – work through them with either dedicated yune practices or, for lighter resistances, continued imagination with an element of *taking in* the imagined experiences and your reactions to them.

I invite you to take a moment and try out a few of these variations on kavek practice now. If you choose to try imagining something you do not want, I recommend imagining what you do want relating to the same subject afterwards so that you can include a positive element in your practice to balance the negative.

Intend (Kavos 2.2)

Finally, we have the kavos (2.2) intending practice. Though all the practices are intentions, kavos refers to the *direct intention of an improved emotional-spiritual state*. The feeling (yunem 1.1), observing (yunor 1.2), and imagining (kavek 2.1) practices all improve one's state through a method that is, to some degree, indirect. In yune practices, we intend to receive and thus become more aware of whatever the present moment reality of our state is. In imagination (2.1) practice, we are asked to expand our awareness of the possibility space of different states and external conditions. All of these practices produce greater awareness and create improvements to our emotional-spiritual state as a byproduct.

In kavos (2.2) practice, we intend *directly* to be in the state we desire. How is this accomplished? It is simply an intention like moving your hand in the physical world.

Chapter Four • The Tree of Practices

Usually, the trouble is not so much that we do not know how to do this but rather that barriers or resistances are in our way. When we go to intend something, we encounter barriers, and often give up, concluding that we must not have the power of choosing to be in the state we desire.

By incorporating a diverse and encompassing set of practices, the Adoga framework provides a remedy to this situation. We can use kavos to bring up the barriers to a state and then address these barriers with the other practices. When there are no barriers to being in a certain state, creating it is often as easy as moving your hand.

While eliminating barriers is crucial, we can also tackle the problem from a different angle by using kavek imagination practice to explore and learn *how* to be in a desired state. Initially, we may not have a feel for how a desired state works or even what it really is, but through imagination practice we can clarify what a state is, what is required to be there, and what it means for our lives.

When supported by all of these practices, kavos intention can be powerful. To test out this practice, select a specific state that you want to experience – perhaps peace, excitement and passion, appreciation or joyfulness, or something else altogether. Then, intend it. Don't overthink it. It is simple. Ask for it. Commit to yourself that this is what you want. And then do the thing. Be at peace. Be joyful. Get excited. But then, of course, be prepared for the barriers to arise because arise they will.

Once again, return to one of the yune practices when a significant amount of resistance arises. When the resistance is mostly eliminated, return to the intention of creating your desired state. Do this repeatedly, and over time you will manifest your intention.

Receiving and Creating Revisited

Now that we have covered the practices on the four-part level of division – yunem feeling (1.1), yunor observing (1.2), kavek imagining (2.1), and kavos intending (2.2) – we can reexamine yune receiving (1) and kav creating (2) in a new light. Yune receiving and kav creating are their own unique practices, not just categories to put other practices in. This raises the questions "What makes yune receiving distinct from yunem feeling or yunor observing?" and (along the same lines) "What makes kav creating distinct from kavek imagining or kavos intending?"

To review, in yunem feeling we are seeking to become aware of the truth of our own experience. In yunor observing, we are seeking to become aware of the observing self and thus free ourselves of any limitations in our current experience. Considering this, the practice of yune receiving is an intention to both become aware of your experience while also finding freedom from it at the same time. This feels like a *broader process* where you are both taking in your experience as well as releasing your attachment to it. It has a simultaneous taking in and letting go feeling.

For kav creating, there is a similar situation where the intention becomes to both imagine and intend an experience at the same time. This looks like imagination with direct intention to manifest what you are imagining. Kav creating also has the feeling of a broader process where you are both taking in imaginative potential and enacting that potential at the same time.

Adoga Practices From Yune to Kav

Yunem (1.1) is nonselective. It takes in whatever experience wants to come through. In this way, it is general, focusing its attention toward all the possibilities of the emotional-spiritual domain. In contrast, kavos (2.2) narrows its attention on one specific state. Often, the narrower and more specific we can make our intended state, the more clarity we will have and the greater ability we will have to manifest our intentions. Kavos intending is therefore selective. It requires experience to be one way – the selected way – but not another way.

In the middle of the tree, we can see how yunor (1.2) provides a little bit more specificity in comparison to yunem (1.1) through its emphasis on focus. Kavek (2.1) then goes one step further by focusing on specific envisioned experiences. And then these envisioned experiences are narrowed into further specificity by the kavos (2.2) process, which selects what experiences we want to manifest.

The progression from yune to kav is, in one perspective, the progression from the nonselective to the selective. This progression represents a spectrum moving from a space that is open to oneness, to the totality of possibility space, receptive to all voices, opinions, and thoughts, to a space that is focused and energized toward a singular vision, expressive and creative, seeking to manifest potentials that originate from its complementary opposite.

Cultivating the Practices

There are many significant orders of ados. Ordering the practices from yune to kav, we can see the progression from generality and receptivity to specificity and expression. However, the order 1.2, 1.1, 2.1, 2.2 allows us to discover the ados in a way that creates maximal contrast and thus clear definition.

Now, I'll introduce a third order of these ados designed to facilitate the ideal learning and cultivation of these practices over time. The recommendation is to start with yunor (1.2), progress to kavek (2.1), followed by yunem (1.1), and lastly arrive at kavos (2.2). You can experiment with focusing on different centers of subtle energy for each of these practices. You can feel (1.1), observe (1.2), imagine (2.1), or intend (2.2) an experience located in a specific center or in the breath. I also recommend becoming familiar with simple imagination before progressing on to more complex forms of imagination.

Once you become familiar with practices on the four-part level of division, you'll be an ideal to position to

Chapter Four • The Tree of Practices

work on cultivating the practices on the two-part level of division, integrating your experience with yunem (1.1) and yunor (1.2) into the yune (1) practice and integrating your experience with kavek (2.1) and kavos (2.2) into the kav (2) practice.

Consider that you can perform these practices in dedicated sessions of self-growth practice or as a background process in day-to-day life. I recommend starting with dedicated sessions to get a feel for a practice. Once you understand the essence of a practice, you can begin to use it while doing other simple tasks. For example, you can try to stay in touch with your emotional-spiritual state, continuously receiving (1) its fluctuations while you cook a meal or do laundry. You might also try imagining (2.1) or intending (2.2) a positive emotional-spiritual state while having a conversation.

Chapter Five
The Tree of Rest

In Ado Theory, we are concerned with balance. In particular, we are concerned with balancing holans so that we may obtain the most encompassing understandings possible. In the last chapter, we covered the tree of practices – the things we do in Adoga. Here, we will cover the tree of rest – that of non-doing, if you will. In other words, the last chapter was dedicated to the intentions of Adoga, whereas this chapter will be dedicated to the release of intentions.

These forces – doing and non-doing, intention and non-intention, activity and rest – must balance each other and support each other in a healthy system. Intention, in both conscious and subconscious forms, creates our emotional reality. Non-intention is the means by which emotional-spiritual energy is released back into potential or, in other words, the means by which it is eliminated. This perspective reveals the immense importance of rest. If positive emotions are created most directly through intention, then negative emotions are released or healed most directly through rest or the release of intention. Rest generates potential. The experience of tiredness indicates low inner potential and the need for rest.

In dedicated self-growth sessions, we can intentionally use rest to release old emotional-spiritual

Chapter Five • The Tree of Rest

energy and integrate new energy. I always begin a session of Adoga with rest. The reason being that I want to release any built up unnecessary intentions before creating new ones through the practices of Adoga. It is like clearing the slate. And anytime I get confused, overwhelmed, or I'm just not sure what to do next, I come back to a baseline of simply resting and releasing. Rest is also a useful tool at the end of a session of self-growth for integrating and processing any changes that have occurred throughout your work.

Outside of dedicated sessions, restful activities like sleeping, eating, relaxing, having space and processing time, and self-care habits serve the vitally important functions of recovery and restoration.

We can create an ado tree where each ado represents a different form of rest. Exploring this possibility space will enable you to release and thus be free of old patterns and energies more powerfully and intelligently.

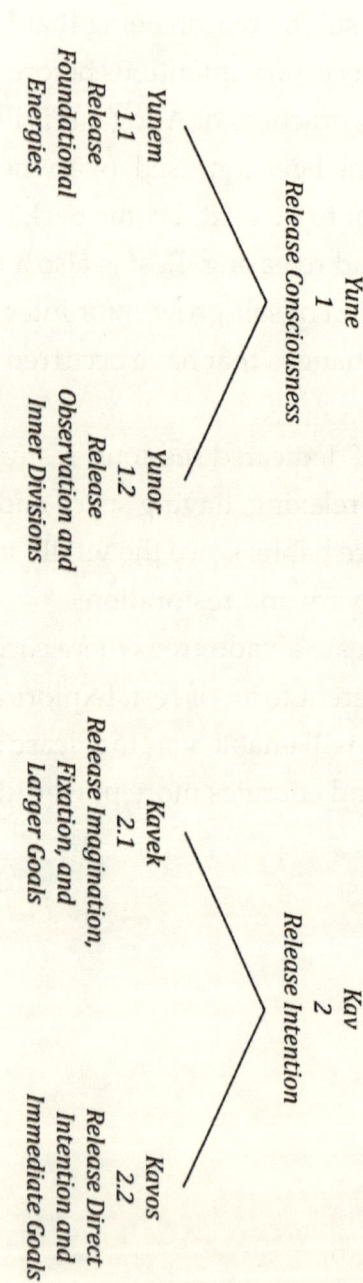

In this chapter, we will discuss each of the forms of rest on the previous page, this time moving from kav to yune. This will create a progression from the "lighter" forms of rest to the "deeper" forms of rest. We'll begin with holans based on the two-part division, and then we will proceed to the holans based on the four-part division.

Release Intention (Kav 2)

In the last chapter, we used conscious intention to move our hands through the possibility space of movement. By being aware of the intending self and sensing its presence, you can then consciously relax its hold on your energy. You can return your energy, the effort of intending, into a yune state of potential. To do this, you will need to release your focus. When you are resting in this way, the sense of potential may be palpable. You may feel that you could be doing more than what you are doing and this is fine. *In fact, this is the essence of rest.* By resting you will create new potential for future intentions, which is the important function this aspect of life serves.

Release Consciousness (Yune 1)

As rest deepens, we may unmanifest or relax not just our intention but also our consciousness or awareness. Consciousness shifts from experiencing the external and formed world to experiencing the internal and formless world. The more we are aware of formlessness, the more our rest intensifies. In the deepest forms of rest, we are no longer expending any energy perceiving the formed world but instead are consumed in a state of simple being within a field of potential.

Release Direct Intention and Immediate Goals (Kavos 2.2)

Looking at this same spectrum on the four-part level of division, kavos describes the relaxation of direct intentions and immediate goals. This area of the spectrum may naturally come to mind through the simple intention "relax." Here, we let go of any goals that we might be striving toward. Keep in mind that you can also bring these goals back into forefront of your mind, if you so choose. When the kavos level of consciousness has been relaxed, a kavek imaginative or dreamy state will naturally emerge.

Release Imagination, Fixation, and Larger Goals (Kavek 2.1)

This area of the spectrum reveals the possibility of relaxing the imagination and mental activity. You may find the intention of releasing the fixations of the mind particularly helpful. When mental focus is released, you can then allow the general (now unfocused) activity of the mind to quiet down in increasing levels of depth. Here, our larger life goals and values unmanifest themselves into a pliable state, open to change. When the kavek level of consciousness is relaxed, a yunor, quiet yet present, restful state emerges.

Release Observation and Inner Divisions (Yunor 1.2)

Here we get in touch with the effort required to divide consciousness into observer and observed. We can then relax the consciousness present in our observing self into potential, releasing our awareness into a yunem state of simple and fundamental energies. This form of relaxation also includes the release of resistances. We let go of the energy it takes to wall off any emotional energies we are storing in the subconscious. As these walled off energies come to the surface, you'll arrive at a unified state where the conscious and subconscious mix.

Release Foundational Energies (Yunem 1.1)

Here, we are in touch with the most foundational, basic energies of the self. The yunem form of relaxing allows these foundational energies to dissipate and return to potential. When the yunem level of the self is released, we find ourselves in an empty state of pure potential. In such a deeply relaxed state, we are in ideal position to make lasting, structural changes to our consciousness.

Chapter Six
The Tree of Emotions

In this chapter, we will look at the ado tree in the context of emotions or, more broadly speaking, emotional-spiritual states. At this point, we are turning our attention away from intention and the release of intention and toward the creations of intention – a territory of emotional, mental, and spiritual forms. After covering all fours trees, we will see how the trees of emotion and thought inform our practice and rest, creating a deeper and richer system of self-growth.

In the previous chapters, we have looked at the two and four-part levels of division. In this chapter, we will move on to the eight-part level of division for the first time. In addition, I'll describe each ado on the eight-part level of division in terms of positive (desirable) and negative (undesirable) aspects. This method allows us to define each ado as a quality on the spectrum from yune to kav, which is neither inherently good nor bad. Instead, each ado describes a variety of experience and corresponding processes. Each ado can represent a response to a perceived positive or negative event. And each can represent a healthy or unhealthy internal process.

See the tree on page 100 for a visual representation of the tree of emotions. We will be concentrating our efforts on the eight-part level of division this chapter, so I have included brief descriptors of the positive and negative qualities of each ado on this level of the tree. Keep in mind that these are only initial indicators toward the flavor of each ado. Deeper definitions and descriptions of each ado will be discussed throughout this chapter.

Part Two • The Four Trees of Adoga

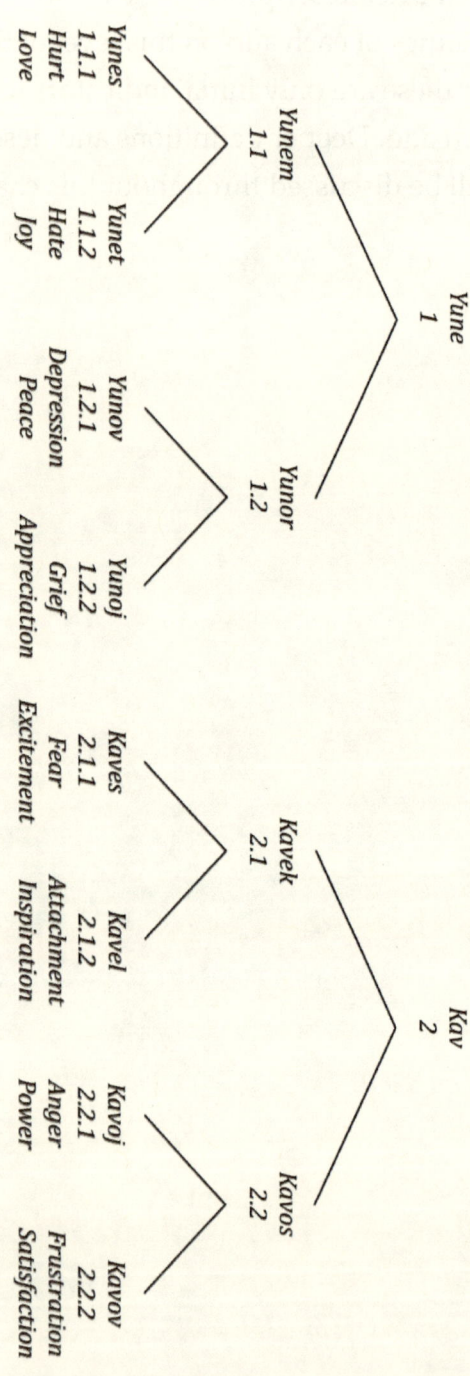

```
Yune
 1
├── Yunem 1.1
│   ├── Yunes 1.1.1 — Hurt / Love
│   └── Yunet 1.1.2 — Hate / Joy
└── Yunor 1.2
    ├── Yunov 1.2.1 — Depression / Peace
    └── Yunoj 1.2.2 — Grief / Appreciation

Kav
 2
├── Kavek 2.1
│   ├── Kaves 2.1.1 — Fear / Excitement
│   └── Kavel 2.1.2 — Attachment / Inspiration
└── Kavos 2.2
    ├── Kavoj 2.2.1 — Anger / Power
    └── Kavov 2.2.2 — Frustration / Satisfaction
```

The negative polarities of each ado can represent challenges and instability, which may lead to positive change further down the road. Or they may become traps that halt and hinder progress. Although negative polarities do represent problems and challenges, they can also potentially be healthy in their own way. Negative emotions serve as a natural warning mechanism that tells us that something is not as it should be. The specific variety of negative emotion will give us information about what the nature of the problem is, and this is a useful and healthy function. Therefore, eliminating negative emotions and states altogether is not necessarily the goal. Rather we will focus more on developing a healthy relationship with our negative emotions, understanding what they mean and what they might have to teach us. In parallel, we can also focus on developing the capacity to deeply experience and powerfully utilize the positive emotions and states.

The holans on the tree of emotions are best understood in relationship to one another. For this reason, we'll look at two holans at time, including positive and negative aspects of each. By doing this we can make comparisons both between the positive and negative polarities of emotions as well as adjacent positions to the left or right on the tree. For this chapter, we will proceed from yune to kav. I have entitled each section with a negative descriptor of the given ado followed by a positive one, with associated general ado names and tree language in parenthesis.

Hurt-Love (Yunes 1.1.1) and Hate-Joy (Yunet 1.1.2)

Yunes (1.1.1) and yunet (1.1.2) relate to yunem (1.1) and the process of feeling, in particular feeling in an undivided and immersive kind of way. As states, I like to think of yunes and yunet as *essential emotions* in the sense that they revolve around the essence of our feelings prior to being shaped and formed by higher levels of complexity.

When dealing with emotional-spiritual states, we will find that the characteristic of inwardness is important to yune holans, whereas worldliness or outwardness is important to kav holans. For example, negative yunes describes an inwardly directed and raw hurt, whereas negative yunet describes hate and blame with a degree of focus on external objects (such as people, ideas, or things that you hate or blame). We can see in this relationship how yunet adds greater specificity, when compared with yunes, by focusing the feeling on defined objects.

Negative yunes is the emotion that responds to the failure of meeting the essential and fundamental needs or wants of the self. We are hurt when the essence of our situation is not what we need or want. Commonly, negative yunes arises when we are perceiving a lack of love, connection, or safety. Negative yunet is also related to essence, but now it is directed toward specific objects. We *hate* things that seem to be essentially and fundamentally bad. It could be that we hate an external object in the world or a specific and defined aspect of our self. Negative yunet can also look like a *bad attitude* – a negative disposition that is broadly applied due to its generally yune nature and yet still focuses its energy somewhat into specific channels and worldly objects.

On the positive side, yunes is described as love. It is a unifying and inclusive emotion. It also represents the successful meeting of basic needs like connection and safety. Yunet is like child-like joy, a more expressive and active emotion, moving slightly toward the external. Positive yunet may take on a specific focus, in much the same way as negative yunet, as in finding joy in a specific activity or finding joy in a certain environment. In contrast, positive yunes is unconditional and general. It expresses the sentiment that all things are deserving of its kind embrace.

Another lens we can use to understand these states is that of *shame* (1.1.1) and *guilt* (1.1.2). These emotions, like hurt and hate, relate to how we perceive the essence of things. Psychologically, this may concern our perception of identity issues, whether we think of ourselves or others as being fundamentally good, bad, shameful, deserving, undeserving, and so on. We will revisit this topic in the next chapter, but for now, it may be helpful to note that the negative yunes can also take the form of shame and negative yunet can also take the form of guilt. Guilt is more kav than shame because it adds the specificity of being guilty *about* defined things, events, failings, and so on. Shame, on the other hand, as we mean it in this context, is directed more generally. We feel shame not about an aspect of ourselves but about our self as a whole. From there, shame spreads into our experience of everything.

In the context of emotional-spiritual states, I use the descriptors hurt and hate most commonly for the negative polarities of the 1.1.1 and 1.1.2 positions respectively. I feel that these words get to how these emotions *feel* the most effectively. Negative yunes *feels* like a hurting sensation. And along the same lines, the feeling of negative yunet is easily recognizable by a general bad attitude and hateful energy. The terms *shame* and *guilt* are more useful from a mental or psychological perspective.

All the emotions in the yunem (1.1) area of the tree are heart-centric. They are basic, vulnerable feelings. These are feelings that often get repressed away and, sadly, often never get to see the light of day. In the negative states, the experience can be like a *heartache*. In the positive states, the experience may feel like a *heart warmth* – a kind of flowing and glowing energy.

Depression-Peace (Yunov 1.2.1) and Grief-Appreciation (Yunoj 1.2.2)

Yunov (1.2.1) and yunoj (1.2.2) relate to the yunor (1.2) area of our tree and the process of observing. The states of yunov and yunoj build upon the foundation of the essential constructs we discussed in the previous section. In the yunor (1.2) area of the tree, we add focusing processes and dualistic qualities. Here, the observer is born.

Focus is an immensely useful capacity, but it comes

with a potential downside – *repression*. We have talked about repression before along with the related concepts of resistance and barriers, but now we can define these terms more fully. The process of focused observation allows us to remove ourselves from parts of our experience. In a positive sense, this can create a sense of perspective and freedom from our limitations. In the negative sense, separation can eliminate parts of our experience from our awareness, either partially or entirely, creating what we call *repression*. Repression either hides or distorts parts of our experience. It represents a lowering of our awareness. Literally, a lesser amount of experience that we are *aware of*. This is, of course, limiting in the sense that we cannot expect to resolve problems that we do not know exist! Nor can we expect to improve our situation in an area that we don't understand in a truthful, accurate, and relatively complete way.

On the other hand, repression is also a natural safe guard with a valid function that should be respected. If you were to experience everything that you could possibly experience in your emotional-spiritual depths all the time, including all the pain, confusion, grief, anger, and shame that exists anywhere within you, there is no doubt that any person's constitution would dissolve into unfunctioning, unproductive mess. No matter how evolved we might be, the emotional-spiritual realm within each of us is endless, boundless. A limit to what we are aware of must be placed *somewhere*. Repression is a natural mechanism for giving us just the right amount of experience, adapting to what we are ready for and what a particular situation calls for. Our job is not to remove the limitation of repression entirely but rather to make sure that our repressing and experiencing mechanisms are healthy and in balance, giving us both the challenge and success we need to thrive.

With this framework of repression in mind, we can begin to make sense of yunor (1.2) states. The negative polarity of yunov (1.2.1) is *depression*. This holan can also include qualities of *numbness, despair, purposelessness,* and *apathy*. It is, in many ways, the quintessential and basic form of repression. This is the condition that results from using focusing power to focus our attention *away* from important aspects of our emotional-spiritual state. The result is that as our focus fixates on something else, our repressed feelings are walled off and isolated. We are left without feelings that should be integrated into our awareness. The result is a sense of numbness. Repression removes the information and passions that emotions provide, leaving us apathetic, low energy, and depressed.

In contrast, positive yunov (1.2.1) is the healthy and growthful version of this same level on the spectrum from yune to kav. Here, division is also created but not in a repressive way. We remain aware of experience on two sides of a divided perception. As an *observer*, we sense the spacious, formless, and deep self that connects to yune and oneness. Our experience also includes an *observed* world, which *remains in awareness*. The removed and unattached observing self provides the opportunity to achieve freedom from the observed world's bondages and suffering. Despite being free and unattached, in a healthy yunor (1.2) state we continue to be connected to, rather than resistant to, the observed world. We *feel* it deeply, continuing to include the awareness of yunem (1.1) while adding the freedom, complexity, and depth of yunor (1.2).

One of the big downsides to repression is that in order to remove aspects of our experience from our awareness we must expend an enormous amount of energy to *resist* the repressed experience. This *resistance* is the energy that fuels the barriers around our repressed experience. You can train yourself to feel or sense resistance. It feels like the emotional-spiritual equivalent of tensing a muscle and indeed is often accompanied by the tensing of physical muscles. You'll know that you have found a resistance if, when you start to relax this tensing energy within your emotional-spiritual space, you begin to experience new emotions, sensations, and awareness as well as an increase in energy, which occurs as the energy you were spending on resistance returns to you as potential.

This illuminates a key difference between negative and positive yunov (1.2.1). Negative yunov includes *resistance* and *tension* and thus is a tired and low-energy state. It is exhausting to keep that resistance up all the time! In contrast, positive yunov is *deeply relaxing*. You feel *okay* about things in a profound way, which allows you to be open and loving. You also have *energy, aliveness,* and *focus* because the energy that you might have spent in resistance is now residing within you as potential, to be used in productive and creative ways throughout your life.

When the yunor (1.2) observing process creates a separation between observer and observed, it also creates an aspect of the self that is more purely yune – the observer – balanced with an aspect of the self that is more purely kav – the observed self. The potential for more purely yune or kav experiences then becomes a distinctive quality to yunor (1.2) states. Yunor is especially defined by the birth of the observer or witness. This observational self is a purified and separated experience of yune qualities like spaciousness, inwardness, oneness, and connectivity. Although yunor (1.2) is more kav than yunem (1.1), it can appear to be the opposite when we focus on the extremely yune observer or witness. However, we must keep in mind that this extreme yune is made possible through a foundational, kav process of separation.

Positive yunov (1.2.1) is an experience of having perspective and with that sense of perspective comes the empowerment of independence and freedom. In negative yunov (1.2.1), the experience is characterized by a distance that feels limiting rather than freeing. Positive yunov can be a deeply spiritual experience, connecting us to the unified infinity that emanates from the most inward aspects of our experience. Negative yunov, then, can often bring a sense of spiritual poverty, perhaps in the form of nihilism or meaninglessness.

Moving into the yunoj (1.2.2) states, the experience again turns slightly more toward the external world. Negative yunoj, which can be described as grief or sadness, focuses on specific or worldly things like something bad that happened, something good you lost, or something bad that is happening or that you are certain will happen. Yunoj focuses on a sense of perspective and how things fit into the bigger picture. In the negative polarity, we either see this bigger picture in a negative light or we are disconnected from its truest nature.

On the positive side, yunoj can be described as appreciation, gratitude, or awe. It is characterized by a positive focus and observation, directed to a specific subject, often a worldly subject, that we are appreciating, that we like, feel grateful for, or feel a sense of awe about. In positive yunoj, the connectivity and oneness of life is seen in *worldly expressions*, in the form of beauty, harmony in complexity, or wonder. Yunoj is a source of wisdom, depth, curiosity, and spirituality.

Fear-Excitement (Kaves 2.1.1) and Attachment-Inspiration (Kavel 2.1.2)

Kaves (2.1.1) and kavel (2.1.2) relate to the kavek (2.1) area of the ado tree and the process of imagination. We now are moving into the kav half of the tree of emotions, and this is marked by a distinct change in flavor. In the kav half, active intention and expressive creativity will come to the forefront. For imagination-oriented (2.1) states, the focus is on *what might happen*. We are concerned here primarily with *potentials*.

When we feel that something bad *might* happen, we

experience anxiety or fear – the negative polarity of kaves (2.1.1). If something bad *does* happen, we will no longer be afraid but instead will experience a state in another area of the spectrum, possibly hurt (1.1.1), sadness (1.2.2), or even anger (2.2.1) or frustration (2.2.2), as we'll cover in the next section. When we feel that something *good might* happen, we experience hope or excitement – the positive polarity of kaves (2.1.1). Likewise, if the good thing *does happen*, the experience will shift to a different area of the spectrum. Because fear and excitement share this potential-focused quality, they feel similar – like a tension or energy building inside. Both fear and excitement are generated in the imagination because the imagination is our natural tool for exploring and relating to potentials.

Kaves is often concerned with the question "What will happen in the world?" In line with our progression to the kav half of the tree, kaves takes on a more worldly flavor in comparison to previous states that were concerned with questions of self-identity, essence, connectedness, and harmony. We can also notice the *active* and *expressive* quality of kaves. Not only is this state about what might happen but also what we might do about it. How could we respond? What are the possibilities? Then, how would the world respond to our response? And so on. These are the kinds of thoughts that naturally arise in a kaves state – all centered in the imagination and in our "head space" rather than our "heart space."

While kaves explores the possibility space of our lives in a free and general way, kavel (2.1.2) begins to focus on just a particular, specific potential or, at least, a more narrow, more specific set of potentials. The negative aspect of kavel can be described as *attachment, obsession,* or *greed.* Negative 2.1.2 represents a lack of flexibility and an unproductive fixation on a particular outcome. Negative kavel might look like sacrificing important values in a process that suffers from an illusory form of "ends justify the means" thinking. Negative kavel states often have a *frantic* or *overactive* feeling.

Transformed into a positive experience, kavel looks like *inspiration* and *passion*. This is the experience we create when we have a specific vision, dream, or goal, but we also have a healthy perspective on our desire. We can balance activity and rest. We incorporate our values as an integral part of our vision and goal, eliminating "ends justify the means thinking" in favor of a passionate commitment to positive and effective means. Part of our vision is a *way of doing things* or a *way of being in the world* that we feel excited about, not just an end result.

Kavel is the area of consciousness where our sense of purpose comes from. This means your overall vision and purpose for your life, your philosophical views on purpose, and your relationship with goals, outcomes, and progressive steps in your day-to-day life. Kavel produces our sense of *why* we are doing what we are doing. What is important? What kinds of pursuits are inspiring and worth putting in the effort to manifest? These are the kinds of questions that are relevant to the mind and heart of kavel.

Anger-Power (Kavoj 2.2.1) and Frustration-Satisfaction (Kavov 2.2.2)

Finally, we come to our last group of emotional-spiritual states. These are the most kav of emotions and states, relating to the kavos (2.2) area of consciousness, the process of direct intention, and our relationship to manifestation.

We can describe the positive aspect of kavoj (2.2.1) as power. It is the state that expresses a high ability to affect manifestation in the ways we desire. Once dreams and desires are formed in the kavek (2.1) area of consciousness, kavoj reflects to us our perceived *potential* in the process manifesting those dreams and desires. Notice how, although kavoj is mostly a kav force with strong interests in the world and manifestation, it also has a small component of potential, representing the last thread of yune before we reach the right-most area of the tree. The feeling of power does not always have to accompany the enactment of power, simply the potential for enactment is enough. Kavoj has the ability to be active but can also be calm, simply accumulating its potential energy.

We can describe the negative aspect of kavoj as anger. It is what we experience when we feel a lack of ability to affect manifestation, a lack of ability to realize our dreams, goals, and desires. When we feel *powerless*, we also feel angry. Anger represents the experience of being *deprived* of abilities and potentials that we desire.

The last position to the right on our tree is named kavov (2.2.2). Here, the focus is specifically on manifestation. Kavov reflects how we feel about what is *here*, what is *now*, what is *in front of us*. When a desire or need is denied, we are *frustrated*. In other words, we are *dissatisfied* with the result. This is the negative polarity of kavov. On the positive side, when a desired outcome is realized or when a need is effectively met, we feel *satisfied*. Positive kavov can be experienced as anything from *pleasure* to *fulfillment*, depending on what kind of need or desire we are responding to. On more primitive, physical levels, we experience pleasure and satiation. On more elevated, emotional, mental, or spiritual levels, we experience states like fulfillment, contentment, or perhaps even simply happiness. This kav area of the spectrum is concerned with the end of processes rather than the beginning. Have we achieved the *end result*, the *direct* and *primary goal* in the *here* and *now*? Kavov states reflect our answer to this question on the emotional-spiritual level.

You might notice that kavov is similar to yunes (1.1.1) in that both are direct responses to successful or unsuccessful meeting of our needs and wants. This interesting similarity may point to the way states come full circle, creating cycles from yune to kav and from kav back to yune. However, there is also an important distinction between kavov and yunes. Kavov is specifically the response we face to the success or failure of our *intentions*. Yunes is a broader awareness of our situation which often includes feelings we are not fully aware of.

Chapter Seven
The Tree of Thoughts

In this chapter, we will examine psychology and the mental realm, especially as it affects emotional-spiritual states. We will break down the mental realm into four ados: essence and identity (yunem 1.1), freedom and possibility (yunor 1.2), purpose and clarity (kavek 2.1), and focus and resonance (kavos 2.2). We will discuss the basic character of each ado and consider positive and negative possibilities in each area of the tree. To end Part Two, I'll present a brief review of the four trees of Adoga, looking at connections between each of the trees in the process.

Chapter Seven • The Tree of Thoughts

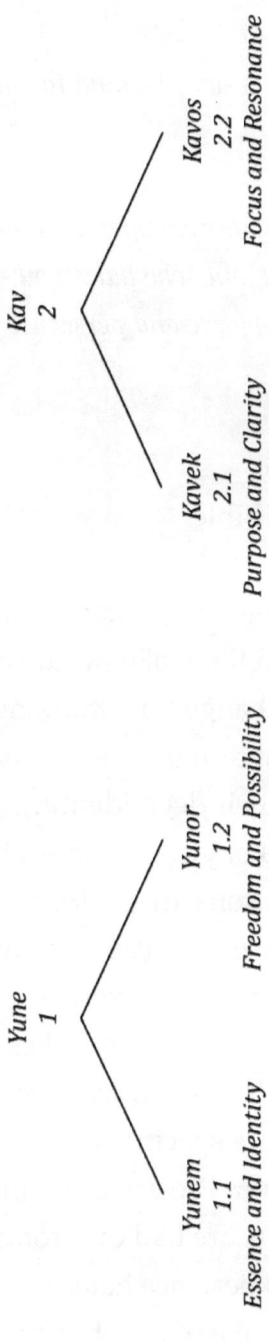

Essence and Identity (Yunem 1.1)

You have heard that it is said, Be kind to your friend, and hate your enemy.

But I say to you, Love your enemies, and bless anyone curses you, and do good to anyone who hates you, and pray for them who carry you away by force and persecute you...

-Matthew 5:43-44
Lamsa Translation of
The New Testament Bible

The thinking of yunem (1.1) is *not* concerned with what things do, what form they take, what variation they are in, or how they might change. The thinking of yunem is concerned with what things *are* – to their core, to their essential nature, to their deep identities.

The questions of yunem can sound simple in a way, though their implications are profound: Am I good? Am I bad? Do I deserve love? Are *you* good or bad or deserving of love? When we perceive ourselves as bad on an *essential level* – bad not just for making mistakes or having flaws, but bad because *that's who you are* – we feel shame. Centered around more specific reasons or events this emotion becomes guilt. Projected out into the world as a perception that others are bad or wrong at the level of their core identities, we experience hate.

A central mistake of negative yunem is the belief in

the permanence of a judgment. Negative yunem says that if you are bad, you are bad permanently and inherently. This perspective eliminates all possibility of growth and therefore is one of the most fundamental errors. Positive yunem, in contrast, is a hopeful mindset that allows us infinite chances to grow and improve. Positive yunem may judge characteristics or actions as good or bad, effective or ineffective, but it does so in a way that facilitates change and growth. It points the way toward what can be transformed and how.

Perhaps most fundamentally, positivity in yunem is characterized by benevolence – a desire for good for yourself and others. Negativity in yunem is characterized by the fundamental flaw of malevolence. The illusion of malevolence says that you should act badly toward those you perceive as acting badly. It says that people must earn your forgiveness, earn your positive emotion or good wishes. In truth, acting badly is bad, regardless of what it responds to. The sensical path is to promote well-being and goodness maximally, in all situations. Only negative emotion makes us stray from this simple and profound truth.

Negative yunem is energized by malevolent or hateful judgment. Positive yunem is energized by unconditional benevolence and forgiveness. Malevolent judgment results in shame, the idea that you are bad in essential and unchangeable ways. "You failed at this endeavor, therefore you are a bad person," is an example of this kind of thinking. Forgiveness is the release and transcendence of such illusions. Forgiveness opens up the possibility of constructive feedback and growth. Only once we think of ourselves as valuable and worthy of hopefulness can we listen deeply to an honest critique – from ourselves or others – and grow in response.

Negative yunem hides under many guises that claim to be acceptable: fairness, justice, the story that punishment, shame, or revenge are righteous and deserved. Often these guises are based on the reasoning that some form of equality justifies our malevolence. For example, consider the idea and emotion of revenge. One might feel that because they have been hurt, they are justified in hurting. The voice of malevolence tries to convince us that creating equality between what has been done to us and what we do to the world is desirable. What happens in practice when people take revenge? It usually leads to more and more revenge. A malevolent action begets a malevolent response and that response creates its own malevolent response, and so on. Generally, these cycles escalate into full on war until one side eliminates the other or perhaps both sides eliminate each other. It seems clear to me that the mindset of revenge is incredibly destructive.

The higher perspective is one of compassionate defense. The benevolent person, one imbued with positive yunem, is not afraid nor hesitant to defend themselves and what they love. If someone tries to hurt you, you may decide to take action to defend yourself in the spirit of positive yunem. Such action can come from a place of

Chapter Seven • The Tree of Thoughts

benevolence if the motivation is to create the most good for all and if the means to achieve that good are compassionate and loving.

Shame, hate, punishment, and even fairness all commonly use the same flawed thinking that we see in this story of revenge and its justification. The fundamental idea that we should strive to create equality between what we do and what we receive is a dangerous idea. This is a distorted version of the deep truth that the universe maintains an inherent balance between what we do and what we receive. When we do good works in the world, we receive positive benefits from many sources, predictable and unpredictable. When we act in malevolence or even ignorance, the opposite holds true. These are natural dynamics that play out in a multitude of ways, whether we want them to or not. The trouble arises when we think it is our job to create or enforce this equality between action and response and, especially, when we think the negativity in the world justifies our own malevolence.

There is a law of universal balance at work here. Let us understand this law with great care. The details of this perspective are critical. If understood correctly, you will find profound truth. If misunderstood even a little, you may find profound falsehood.

The equality between action and reception plays out on a multitude of levels: physical, emotional, mental, and spiritual. If we compare only physical manifestations, we may find inequality. Though when we include the broader perspective of multifaceted, internal and external, truths, balance will be found. For example, if someone steals money from you – let's say in a manner that feels to you completely immoral and unjustified – does this universal law guarantee your money back? Certainly not. Does it guarantee another possession on the physical level that is equal in value? Certainly not. But it does guarantee that if you face the suffering in your life with good intent and with integrity and courage, then you will be rewarded, perhaps only with inner fulfillment, perhaps with external manifestations as well. It does guarantee that if you forgive another, your own emotional burden will be lifted. Your intent, which flows out into the world, is equal to your fulfillment, which you receive as emotions, thoughts, and spiritual experience. And through a myriad of mysterious pathways, the state of your emotions, thoughts, and spiritual experience translates into the manifested circumstances of your life over time.

Even in the face of what seems to be undeserved tragedy, a person in a positive state can find meaning, humor, happiness, and fulfillment. And even in the face of what seems to be an abundance of resources, a person in a negative state can manage to suffer. And so, even in the case of undeserved tragedy, there is still an equality. The former person intends well, and so is happy, regardless of their circumstances and how unfair they may be. And the latter person intends poorly, and so they suffer – their poor intent and poor state will make their external abundance meaningless.

Chapter Seven • The Tree of Thoughts

In addition, the internal and external will begin to align over time as a general tendency. The person in a positive state will be able to improve their external situation, using their emotional-spiritual state as a resource. And the person in a negative state will inevitably destroy their external resources over time. And thus, the universe aligns internal with external. And internal intents align with internal emotions. And external actions align with external reactions. And within and among a great diversity of forms and energies, there is a great balance and harmony between all things.

Positive yunem represents *unconditional* benevolence and *unconditional* forgiveness. It knows that benevolence is not something to be earned. It is a way of life and philosophy about how to behave most effectively in the world. Benevolence and forgiveness produce powerful and energy-rich emotional-spiritual states, whereas hatred and shame produce confused and low-energy states. Therefore, benevolence and forgiveness are not only kinder than hatred and shame, they are more effective as well.

While growing toward greater benevolence and love and forgiveness, it is also important to develop a good relationship with your shame and hate. If we listen lovingly to our shame, we can learn important lessons and calm the negative energies within us. A beneficial practice is to listen to your shame and meet your vulnerable and hurt self with love. When you establish unconditional benevolence with yourself, you can consider if there is any truth in your shame. You can ask if any piece of your old shame can be transformed into new constructive criticism that can be used as the basis of growth. Alternatively, you might decide that your shame has no basis in reality and can be let go of entirely without the need to respond to it in any other way. In a similar way, you may find that your hate can be transformed into a positive contribution, working toward the opposite of what initially disturbed you. Or you may find that no response is necessary beyond listening to your emotions lovingly and then letting them go.

It takes honesty to work through our shame and emerge more and more deeply into the mindset of unconditional benevolence and positive yunem. When we adopt a forgiving and loving attitude, we can be truthful with others and with ourselves without fear. This is the foundation of constructive criticism and thus the foundation of growth.

Positive yunem cultivates the virtue of loving empathy. When we can see life from another person's perspective, we will begin to understand that people are always working toward their conception of the good and their mistakes are always caused by a lack of awareness or resource. Even when people act selfishly, apathetically, or malevolently, these mistakes all come from a limitation in understanding and inner resource. When we understand the cause of such limitation, we can forgive it. And when we can forgive, we can act more compassionately and more effectively.

Freedom and Possibility (Yunor 1.2)

"I could never accomplish that." "Yeah, it sucks, but that's just the way it is." "That's just the way it has always been." "Oh well. Watcha gonna do?" "Be realistic." "Be practical." "Don't be silly."

These are the voices of depression – despair hidden away underneath layers of repression. These are the voices of people or aspects of one's self that are not in touch with their virtuous freedom. These are voices that have limited their possibility space in unhealthy ways. These are the voices of negative yunor (1.2).

The voices of positive yunor express freedom and expansive potential:

"What are the probabilities of different outcomes?" "Why are things the way they are?" "How has history shaped the current reality?" "What could the future look like?" "What can I do to make life better for myself and others?" "I can do this." "I am free."

The observational process gives us perspective on our behavior and reality. Without perspective, we are enmeshed in our habits, comfort zones, and patterns. We do things and experience things without realizing that there are alternatives, without even realizing what we are doing or what our experience means. Like a fish swimming in water, a lack of contrast generates a lack of meaning. Perspective provides this meaning-generating contrast and thus allows us to navigate through life more effectively. When we have perspective, we have freedom.

Generally, *limiting* thinking is indicative of yunor problems. *Free, flexible, adaptive,* and *creative* thinking is indicative of yunor virtues.

Questioning habits and assumptions big and small is a central intellectual practice of yunor. For an early agrarian society, this might have meant questioning if sacrificing animals to the gods really improved the harvest. For a Civil War–era United States, this might have meant questioning the morality of enslaving African American people. For Galileo, it meant questioning that the sun revolved around the earth. A man of today might wonder why he is shaving every day. A woman might wonder who first started wearing high heels and why. We might wonder how it came to be that dresses were traditionally worn by women but not men. We might wonder why a suit is "formal" and what "formality" actually means. We might wonder if visual art must imitate realistic situations in life. We might wonder if music must have a beat. We might wonder what makes a liquid a liquid rather than a solid. We might wonder how many miles it is to the sun. We might wonder what technology will be like in twenty years. One might wonder if it is possible to increase their productivity by a factor of five or ten or twenty. You might wonder if it is possible to develop skills that you have never imagined as accessible to you before. We might wonder a lot in yunor thinking.

It is a liberated space of curiosity where we don't pretend to have all the answers, but we certainly have questions. This is the area of thinking where we are challenged to *ask better questions* and, sometimes, to simply ask more questions. To increase our questioning capacity, we must dare to ask the hard questions, the ridiculous questions, the strange questions. We must have the freedom and courage to think and say and ask things that others feel are unsafe to think and say and ask. The key here is that we are not committed to particular answers at this stage of thinking. We are committed to truth and the pursuit of truth. We are committed to the process of curiosity and learning.

In generating new questions, our guiding principle is to expand the possibility space of our thinking. We want to ask things that we have never thought to ask before.

Purpose and Clarity (Kavek 2.1)

In yunor thinking, we expand our awareness of possibility space through questioning and challenging our assumptions. Now, in kavek (2.1) thinking, we are tasked with the challenge of deciding *where we want to go in this expanded possibility space*. A central insight here is that getting to our desired destination is a lot easier when we know what the destination is. The more deeply and clearly we understand the endpoint of a goal, the more empowered we are to achieve that goal. Purpose brings energy, clarity, and meaning to life. Without purpose, life is lifeless. It is dull and lacking. It is no life at all. Purpose makes you alive.

As is characteristic of kav, specificity is important in kavek thinking. Notice how the goal of "creating a good life" might be sincere, but it is not very useful. It does not tell us anything about what a good life looks like. A good purpose addresses the components of a good life, thus illuminating what specific things we need to work toward and what processes we need to use. A good purpose also specifies what is *important* and what is merely minutiae. It helps us to prioritize.

The concept of purpose plays out on both big-picture and detailed levels. In the most general sense, purpose relates to our perspective on what things are most important in the world as a whole. Here we must consider our personal philosophy and relationship with significance and meaning. What matters in life? Is it possible for things to matter and, if so, what makes them matter? Getting a bit more specific, we can ask what *our personal purpose* is. How do we personally fit into the vision of life's design? And finally, most specifically, purpose relates to why we do what we do on an everyday level. What is the purpose of the tasks, habits, and goals that you work on day-to-day?

Kavek thinking asks us to constantly become conscious of our desires. It asks us to envision to the best possible scenarios that we want to move toward and the worst possible scenarios we want to move away from. We can also ask what makes a scenario the worst or the best? What is important to us that has been successful in the ideal scenario or failed in the negative scenario?

A kavek practice is to create and continually refine a list or model of your values. What general goals in life are most important to you? As you refine this list or model of values over time, continually seek to encapsulate more and more of the complexity of life into simple key words or phrases. If you can find quick ways to reference your most important values, you can facilitate the efficient and powerful manifestation of these values in your life.

Focus and Resonance (Kavos 2.2)

...what I feel I create
I am choosing wisely
Where my point of attraction is
Launching rockets of desire
I am calling it in
My dreams are manifesting

And I receive
All that is lined up for me
I receive
And I know that the universe loves me
And that there is nothing I need to prove
It's safe to be me
It's my birthright to feel this happy and free
Oh I receive

An excerpt from the lyrics of "Receive" by Fia

Yunem (1.1) essence and identity psychology establishes a foundation in honesty. In kavos (2.2) thinking, we can consider the effects of a *positive* or *negative focus* within the context of honesty, truthfulness, and accuracy. One can think about truthful and positive things all day or one can think about truthful and negative things all day. We don't want to avoid negative things that should be addressed. But on the other hand, dwelling on negativity, especially if you aren't productively working toward a resolution to the problems you are pondering, takes a toll on your emotional-spiritual state, resulting in a lessened ability to be creative and productive. And this is where the power of *positive focus* is applicable. If we direct our thoughts toward things that we are grateful for and solutions that emanate from and inspire the virtue of hope, our emotional-spiritual state will respond, creating more positive and useful emotions, awareness, and energetic potential.

A core concept in kavos psychology is what I like to call *resonance*. Resonance refers to an analogy that compares vibrations in the physical world to interactions in the emotional, mental, and spiritual realms. In the physical world, when sound waves encounter an object, the object will vibrate if the sound waves match the object's *natural resonance frequency*, as it is called. In the nonphysical sense, when two people argue or fight, we could think of their emotional-spiritual energies as forming a *resonance*. In other words, their psychologies are *aligned* in such a way as to allow them to interact and amplify one another.

We can also find resonance *between* physical and nonphysical domains. For example, placebos create physical benefits based on the nonphysical belief that we are being assisted or healed. In a similar way, we could see how, if someone simply *believed* they were a runner, they might start running because that's what they think runners do. And if this goes on, they slowly will become more and more like a real runner.

Of course, an internal belief cannot completely replace the external reality. When faced with a disease, we would probably rather take the real medication than the placebo. When the runner goes out for that first run, they will probably not be a strong runner despite their belief. Nevertheless, the *tendency* for forms or energies in the different domains – physical, emotional, mental, and spiritual – to start to align over time is an important observation.

We can think of this observation as the *principle of resonance*. The recommendation here is not to try really hard to believe you are runner when you aren't nor to convince yourself that sugar tablets will cure your disease. While insightful, these examples do not respect the foundation of yunem truthfulness and honesty. We need to have an accurate and honest perception of reality. If there are real problems, we must address them. However, within the context of truth, we can explore ways to cultivate more positivity in our mindset.

How often do you appreciate the miracle of being alive? Have you thought about the awe-inspiring complexity of your own brain recently? Do you notice the beauty of the sunset or the birds gliding upon the passing breeze? Do you appreciate the food that you eat or the air you breathe? Have you considered what an incredible gift technology can be, allowing us to communicate near instantly and have near instant access to an unthinkable amount of information with a now common smartphone? Do you think about the immense speeds that the car or airplane you might find yourself in make possible and what our ancestors would have thought of such wizardry?

In the section on yunem psychology, I said that striving to create equality between what we do and what we receive is dangerous. The truth is that the universe itself maintains an automatic and inherent balance or equality between what we do and receive. We can actively make use of this principle with kavos psychology by creating an emotional-spiritual state that resonates with what we want to receive. For example, let's say you want to travel around the world, but doing so seems impossible. You can imagine traveling around the world. You can cultivate the emotions and energetic states that connect you to this vision: curiosity, wonder, exploration, awe, experimentation, investigation, growth. You can discover your resistances to aspects of the vision and then let them go. Using self-growth practices, you can create a state that resonates with your goal. And once you are in a state that resonates with your goal, the manifestation process will flow easily. You will naturally create or receive the resources you need, the ideas you need, the help you need, the courage you need. As you focus on what you want again and again, its energy permeates deeper into your soul; it becomes part of who you are, dispelling what is not compatible and nourishing what is.

Perhaps, a passion for exploration drives you to take a small trip, just to a neighboring town for a night. It didn't seem worthwhile before, but now your state has given you energy and an open mind. There, you happen to meet a new friend who also likes traveling. Now, the two of you talk about traveling incessantly and the vision occupies even more of your thoughts. You learn about an opportunity to travel inexpensively through a friend of your friend and suddenly you are starting to live your dream. You go on a bigger trip, read a book about traveling, do research, learn skills while on your first big trip, and so on. Then, you have more opportunities. And as you travel, your state creates more and more opportunities and resources to keep giving you the experiences that align with your vision. In this way, your internal and external worlds come into alignment over time.

Suffering creates the negative version of this process. As we focus more on what we fear or what we hate, we bring these things into our hearts, our energies, our actions, and then eventually into our circumstances. Imagine, for example, that you discover that a local business is acting unethically. You ruminate on this and obsess over it. You begin to complain about the business with your friends, using the shock-value as entertainment. Over time, more and more people talk about this business.

They gain publicity. The original criticisms are sometimes lost in the process or, perhaps, create many interpretations of events. And, ironically, the increased attention gains them more business. "There's no such thing as bad publicity," as they say. Meanwhile, the more you complain about the situation, the worse you feel, and the less ethically you act. And the worse the people around you feel, and the less ethically they act. And, in a multitude of ways, all things related to the object of your focus are intensified.

Here's an alternate example that distills the essence of this lesson: While bike riding, you become so fearful and focused on the tree ahead of you that you crash straight into it. If you, instead, focus on the path you want to take, you will likely obtain the desired result.

A Summary of the Four Trees of Adoga

We have now completed our initial survey of *the four trees of Adoga* – the tree of practices, the tree of rest, the tree of emotions, and the tree of thoughts. In this section, I will review the material we have covered thus far and help paint a picture of how all these trees relate to one another. Here we can begin to integrate the ados of each tree into larger, more encompassing definitions.

Yunem (1.1) relates to the essence and identity of things, as we have learned from the tree of thoughts. Yunem emotions and states, then, reflect how we feel about the essence of both external things and our own

Chapter Seven • The Tree of Thoughts

identity. Hurt and shame (yunes 1.1.1), as well as hate and guilt (yunet 1.1.2), reflect negative judgments of essence, whereas forgiveness (yunem 1.1), love (yunes 1.1.1), and joy (yunet 1.1.2) reflect positive ones. Essence is foundational, representing the simplicity of the beginnings of holarchy. Therefore, the yunem practice of feeling is the practice of receiving in a unified way. It is the practice of simple, undivided, immersive connecting. In the tree of rest, yunem represents the release of essential and foundational energies.

Yunor (1.2) relates to observation as a separated and unattached witness. An unattached witness is free to explore possibilities due to their separation from the observed, hence the yunor psychology of freedom and possibility. Yunor emotions and states, then, reflect how we feel about our freedom and the possibilities of our life and the world. When possibilities feel trapping and limiting we feel forms depression (yunov 1.2.1), sadness (yunoj 1.2.2), and grief (yunoj 1.2.2). When we have the flexibility to navigate diverse possibilities effectively, we find stability (yunov 1.2.1), balance (yunor 1.2), peace (yunov 1.2.1), and appreciation for the complex beauty of all that we can experience (yunoj 1.2.2). The processes of yunor create the initial divisions within the self, and thus yunor as a form of rest is the release of initial divisions.

In kavek (2.1), we imagine possibilities as a practice. This leads us to the emotions and states that deal with potentials: anxiety and fear (kaves 2.1.1), hope and excitement (kaves 2.1.1), attachment and fixation (kavel

2.1.2), and inspiration (kavel 2.1.2). Psychologically, potentials create desires for the future. When we intellectually prioritize and interrelate our desires, we arrive at a sense of purpose. In the tree of rest, we relax all these imaginative processes.

Finally, we come to kavos (2.2) and the practice of direct intention. Here our emotions and states respond to the potentials and realizations of our intention. When we are deeply in touch with the potentials of our intention, we feel powerful (kavoj 2.2.1). When that power is corrupted by negativity, it becomes anger (kavoj 2.2.1). When intentions achieve desired results, we feel satisfaction (kavov 2.2.2), and when they fail to achieve desired results, we feel frustration (kavov 2.2.2). Psychologically, our direct intention controls our mental focus. And in the tree of rest, we can release our intention to create potential energy.

In summary, then, yunem (1.1) is concerned with the essence of things as well as unified, immersive experiences. Yunor (1.2) pertains to processes of observation, the creation of a sense of perspective, and how much freedom we have to navigate the possibility space of life. Kavek (2.1) relates to imagined potentials for the future and our sense of purpose. And finally, kavos (2.2) centers on direct intentions and outcomes.

Part III

Methods and Expansions

Chapter Eight
The Methods of Adoga

In this chapter, we will learn four methods of performing the Adoga practice: *alignment method, symmetry method, flexible intention method*, and *fixed intention method*. These methods will integrate and interrelate the four trees.

Alignment Method: Aligning Practice With State

If someone is in a negative kavek (2.1) state, we can infer that the processes and practices of kavek are not being executed in a healthy and beneficial way. In contrast, positive kavek states, like hope and inspiration, indicate a healthy and effective use of kavek processes and practices. We become fearful in a limiting way when we don't use our imagination well. We become inspired when we do.

In general, we can say positive states indicate corresponding processes are going well and negative states indicate they are going poorly. If this is the case, it *makes sense to respond to a negative state with a practice that corresponds to the given area of consciousness*. For example, if we are in a state of fear, we would expect that using an imagination practice to improve our kavek processes will directly and effectively address the negative state we are experiencing. Along the same lines, if we desire, in particular, to cultivate a strong sense of hope or inspiration, a corresponding kavek practice is a logical choice.

This is the paradigm of the *alignment method* of Adoga practice. In this method, we are *aligning* the practice we are performing with our state. We can also think of this alignment as extending to the tree of thoughts. Problems arising from a given area of the tree of thoughts may be addressed by performed corresponding or *aligned* practices. Desired positive abilities and conditions in the mental realm may be cultivated, in the same way, using a practice that aligns with the type of ability or condition you want to create.

The implications of this realization quickly become profound. Alignment method can be summarized as the following process:

1. Notice the quality of your state and thoughts.

2. Categorize your experience according to the tree of emotions and/or the tree of thoughts.

3. Perform a practice that aligns with your emotional, mental, and/or spiritual experience.

4. Repeat from step one in a continuous cycle.

Performing alignment method ensures that we are using the right tool for the right job. It is like an instruction manual that tells you to use a screwdriver for screwing in screws but to use a measuring tape for determining the length of an object. Deepening our discernment in this way can create a dramatically more powerful self-growth practice.

With experience, we even may begin to shift practices *rapidly* in response to changes in our emotional-spiritual state and thought processes. Over time, you can develop an intuitive feel for when you are in a given state and what the appropriate practice is for those conditions. You can also develop the ability to perform the four steps above simultaneously so that you are always keeping a portion of your awareness on your state, while also implementing a practice that aligns with that state at the same time, continuously adjusting as your state changes.

It may be useful to look at the following diagram of the eight pairs of emotions and their associations to the four practices while performing alignment method. I recommend, eventually, memorizing this diagram, so that you can perform this practice more quickly and intuitively.

Chapter Eight • The Methods of Adoga 139

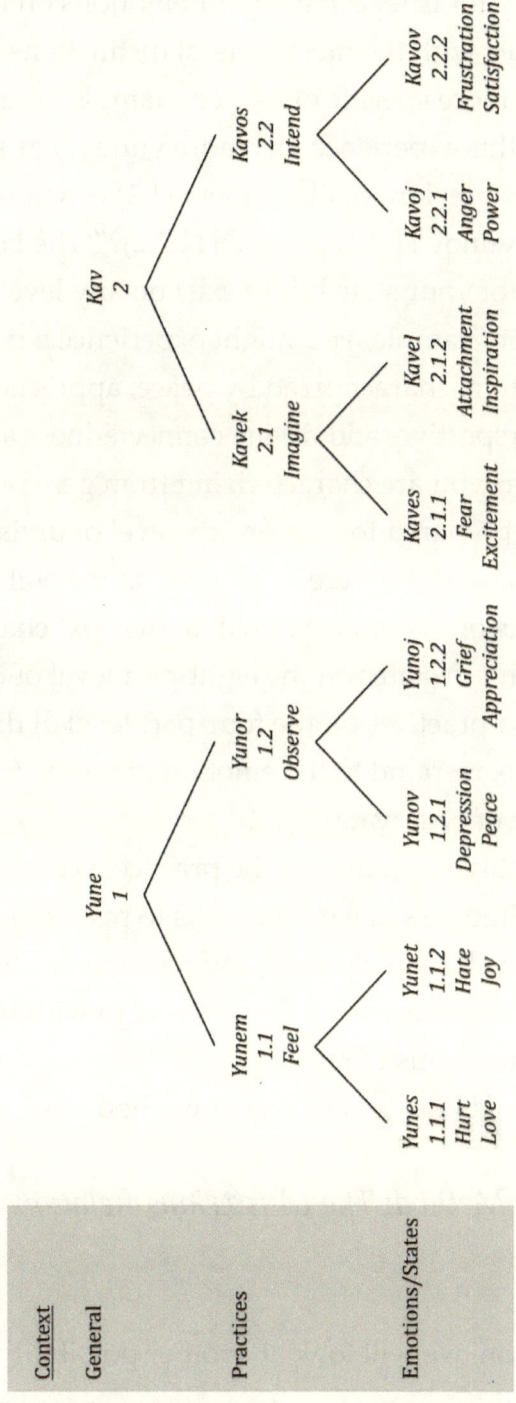

One strategy for categorizing your emotions on the ado tree is to start with the most general distinctions and then progress to more specific ones. For example, you might ask, "Does this experience feel more yune (1) or kav (2)?" Then "Does it feel more like yunem (1.1) or yunor (1.2)?" "More like yunov (1.2.1) or yunoj (1.2.2)?" The best description of your state might exist on any level of division. For example, you might experience a positive yunor emotion, characterized by peace, appreciation, a sense of perspective, and divine connectedness all at once. Therefore, as you are characterizing from general to specific, be prepared to stop on any level of division.

We have not covered practices on the eight-part level of division. Though, we will in the next chapter. For now, respond to states on the eight-part level of division with aligned practices on the four-part level of division. For example, respond to the emotion of yunov (1.2.1) with the practice of observation (1.2).

If at any point during the practice, you experience fatigue or tiredness, the invitation is to rest. In the paradigm of alignment, rest is the response to the state of tiredness. Deeper forms of tiredness align with the deeper or more yune forms of rest.

If you'd like, try alignment method now.

Symmetry Method: The Mysterious Relationships of Symmetry

In this section, we will look at another possibility for

connecting your state to your practice: *symmetry method*. I'll say now that I view the alignment method as the foundation between these two possibilities. I recommend building up experience in the alignment method *first* before progressing on to incorporating symmetry method. In addition, I recommend using alignment method as a response to a specific state experience before using symmetry method within a session of self-growth.

When we talk about symmetry method, we are literally talking about the symmetries that show up in the visual depictions of ado trees. For example, yunoj (1.2.2) has a symmetrical relationship with kaves (2.1.1) because each is only one position to the left or right of the centerline of the tree. Yunov (1.2.1) has a symmetrical relationship with kavel (2.1.2). Yunet (1.1.2) has a symmetrical relationship with kavoj (2.2.1). And, finally, yunes (1.1.1) has a symmetrical relationship to kavov (2.2.2).

These symmetrical relationships have fascinating and significant meaning. Notice how the opposite of depression (1.2.1) seems similar to inspiration (2.1.2). Someone who is hurt (1.1.1) is responding to their needs and desires not being met. Someone who experiences the satisfaction and fulfillment of kavov (2.2.2) is in the opposite situation – they are responding to the successful fulfillment of their needs and desires. Or let's look at two negative states together. Isn't there a sense of commonality between hate (1.1.2) and anger (2.2.1)? Or on the positive side, between joy (1.1.2) and power (2.2.1)? Not all the connections within the symmetries are immediately obvious. Nevertheless, when you investigate these relationships deeply a wealth of wisdom awaits discovery.

In the tree of thoughts, essence and identity psychology (1.1) forms a foundation in honesty and truthfulness. This foundation must be respected to create balance, especially, with focus and resonance psychology (2.2). Freedom and possibility psychology (1.2) is centered on expanding the possibility space; purpose and clarity psychology (2.1) is centered on deepening the possibility space and navigating within it.

In one way, the meaning of symmetry is quite mysterious, but in another way there is a logic to it. 2.1.1 is as kav as 1.2.2 is yune. Though the holans in a symmetrical relationship are different in polarity as either primarily yune or kav, they are similar in their *degree* and thus they *balance each other*. Often it seems that processes and cycles, begin in one holan and then end in the symmetrical holan. We start out in grief (1.2.2) at the loss of an enjoyable environment but then discover a new activity and become excited (2.1.1) about it. We might start out angry and frustrated (2.2) about our external circumstances but then discover the value of going within and finding our inner source of love and joy (1.1). Yune leads to kav and kav leads to yune, and so it goes…

To perform symmetry method, first categorize your experience, just as with the alignment method, but now rather than using the practice that aligns with your experience, use the practice that creates a symmetrical relationship with your experience. As I said before, it is generally advisable to do alignment method first in response to a given experience or state. Sometimes doing an aligned practice will seem to come to a point of completion and yet leave something remaining to be resolved. In this situation, we may benefit from progressing to symmetry method.

This whole process might look like the following example: You examine your experience and notice anxiety (kaves 2.1.1). First, you perform an imagination practice in accordance with the alignment method. You could elect to create a simple imagination or imagine what you do or do not want. You might go through each of these possibilities in turn. After using imagination practices, if you feel that your process has come to an ending point but there is more left to do, you can move on to the symmetrical practice – in this case yunor (1.2) observation. Here, you could elect to observe the mind, the breath, or another constant aspect of your experience, while cultivating your awareness of the spacious and free observing self.

Another example might be that you notice the experience of negative yunes (1.1.1). Here, you would first use feeling (1.1) in accordance with the alignment method and then progress to directly intending (2.2) a positive state in accordance with the symmetry method. If you recognize kavov (2.2.2) in your emotional-spiritual state, the process is reversed, first intention (2.2) and then the symmetrical practice, feeling (1.1).

If you would like, give this a try now, using the

aligned practice first in response to a given experience and then progressing to the symmetrical practice second.

Symmetrical Cycles of Growth

Now that we have seen the basics of how symmetry method operates, let's take a moment to further explore the patterns and principles behind this concept of symmetry.

One key to understanding symmetries is that growth occurs in cycles and that those cycles tend to oscillate in symmetrical patterns. Let's say, for example, that your intention is very active for a period of time. You expend a lot of energy and focus. You perform many activities with high intensity and for a long period of time. After this very active phase, you will need a lot of rest, recovery, and integration. In this example, we can see how a strong kav – an intensely active period – is balanced with a strong yune – a lot of rest, recovery, and integration. If we do not respect this balance, for example, by continuing to be highly active without ever resting, we eventually burn out. We will get stronger and stronger messages that we need to rest, until the rest is forced upon us by disease or ailments of various kinds.

In contrast, a mild period of activity may only need to be balanced by a mild period of rest. The principle we are uncovering here is that a kav of a given *strength* must be eventually balanced by a yune of the same strength. And likewise, this works in opposite direction as well. A deep period of rest will naturally lead to a period of activity. If we attempt to disregard this kind of balance by continuing to rest without ever pushing ourselves to be active, we may become bored or restless, eventually perhaps even suffering from anxiety or depression.

The insights of symmetry are a reflection of this principle of balance. When a mildly kav 2.1.1 challenge arises, a mildly yune solution is called for, much in the same way that a period of mild activity calls for mild rest and recovery.

Let's briefly take a look at how a challenge in each area of the tree of emotions might naturally find a solution in the symmetrical position of the tree.

We can begin with the challenge of yunes (1.1.1) on the far-left side of the tree. In this state, we are not getting our needs and wants met. In addition, we may not even be conscious of what our needs and wants even are. The solution then looks like the satisfaction and fulfillment of kavov (2.2.2) in response to meeting our needs and wants consciously. A yunet (1.1.2) challenge of hate is resolved when we can transform our disdain for the world into kavoj (2.2.1), a power that enables us to work towards improving the problems we were initially disturbed by. A yunov (1.2.1) challenge of depression finds its solution when our despair over our limited possibility space is alleviated by the expansion of our possibility space through imagination. The end result is that where before the depressed person felt purposeless, they now feel the inspiration of kavel (2.1.2). A yunoj (1.2.2) challenge of sadness or grief is alleviated when our fixation on loss is released into the open possibilities of hope and excitement in kaves (2.1.1). A kaves (2.1.1) challenge of ubiquitous fear of the externals of one's environment is transformed by a yunoj (1.2.2) experience of freedom and a corresponding understanding of the big-picture. A kavel (2.1.2) challenge of attachment is alleviated when we can let go of the specific possibility we were clinging to and open ourselves up to the peace and infinite potentiality of yunov (1.2.1). A kavoj (2.2.1) challenge of anger can be transformed when our negative response to our own powerlessness gives way to the nonjudgmental activity of joyful yunet (1.1.2). Finally, a kavov (2.2.2) challenge of frustration can be released when we find the forgiveness and patience of yunes (1.1.1). Here, we can love ourselves and others unconditionally despite the shortcomings we may perceive.

Aligning Practice With Potential Energy

Yune practice is best suited for challenging issues that feel more difficult to approach. Kav practice is best suited for developing the highest levels of mastery over a given area of consciousness. Yune reaches further but doesn't go as deep.

We can think of potential energy in the emotional-spiritual domain as the amount of untapped potential we have to use for intentions. When we are stressed, tired, or overwhelmed, potential energy is low. When we are feeling excited, powerful, bored, restless, or awake, potential energy is high.

This understanding of potential energy gives rise to a viewpoint and strategy that complements alignment method. If we are in tune with our sense of potential energy – from tired, on one end of the spectrum, to energetic and ready, on the other end – then we can align our practice with that state of potential energy. Lower potential energy calls for more yune practice. Higher potential energy calls for more kav practice.

Although this viewpoint lacks the specific insights of aligning your practice with one of the holans on the tree of emotions, it can make the whole process more flowing and intuitive. You'll find that aligning practice with the tree of emotions or aligning practice with potential energy are two ways of thinking about the same reality. When you are in a yune state, experiencing, for example, the peace or depression of yunov, potential is going to feel relatively low. It is part of the experience. But if you are in a kav state, like the excitement of kaves or the power of kavoj, then potential energy will be high.

One way of approaching alignment method is to begin on the yune end of the spectrum, first with relaxing all intentions and then rising up to feeling (1.1). At this point, you can gauge how much energy you feel like you have. If you feel complete with feeling, ready to move on, and energetic, step up to observing (1.2). If you are still energetic and ready, keep going to imagining (2.1) and then to intending (2.2). If at any point, you begin to feel challenge or tiredness, follow your state by dropping down to a more yune practice. In this way, you can continue aligning your practice with the level of energy you feel in your state. If you become tired, confused, or overwhelmed, you can drop down all the way to rest for as long as it takes to rebuild your potential energy to a higher level.

Keep in mind that the goal is not to move your state to a higher energy or more kav level. Rather, we are seeking to align our practice with whatever the natural condition of our state happens to be in a given moment.

Flexible and Fixed Intention

We can think of alignment method and symmetry method as falling under the category of *yune* or *receptive methods* of Adoga, meaning methods that ask you to listen to or notice your experience and then respond in some way based on that information.

In *kav* or *intention-based methods*, we choose practices based on our desires and goals. We will set an *intention* for our practice ahead of time and do our best to follow this intention throughout our session of practice. This intention could include just a single practice, a predetermined progression of practices, or specific variations on a practice, like kavos (2.2) intention directed specifically toward the state of positive kavoj (2.2.1) or observing (1.2) directed specifically toward the energetic center of the head and mind. Our intention might also include the desire to work on a specific life issue, question, or capacity.

We get to deeply exercise our creativity in this type of practice. What we want to focus on is up to us. This is an opportunity to explore your desires and to pursue them with a solid foundation of self-growth tools.

In all intention-based practices, rather than responding to our experience, we stick to our desired intentions and allow our experience to transform, move, and change in response to our intentions.

We can use two variations of the intention-based method: *flexible intention method* and *fixed intention method*. Flexible intention method opens up the option of switching to the alignment or symmetry method upon encountering strong resistances. In this method, we will still focus primarily on our predetermined intentions for the session, only deviating from them when resistances are brought up as a result of the intended practices. In fixed intention method, we will attempt to practice only the predetermined practice or practices of the given session without responding to our state at all, within reason of course.

Fixed intention method can feel a bit like an endurance exercise, perhaps comparable to distance running. Here, we will stop if we feel a sense of incurring *injury*. However, if we are simply tired or uncomfortable, we will aim to keep returning to our desired intention again and again with persistence. And if we become distracted, we gently yet persistently and decisively bring ourselves back to the original intention. This is an important aspect of the possibility space of self-growth.

Focus on a single intention and persistently holding it over time trains both our focus and our ability to powerfully intend our desires.

Flexible intention method, on the other hand, has the advantage of allowing you to work on a particular issue of interest from all angles, actively forming the emotional-spiritual state we desire and also listening to and working through our resistances.

A truly encompassing Adoga practice must eventually, and over time, include a balance of receptive and intention-based methods. Using only the receptive methods – alignment method and symmetry method – will tend to slightly bias your practice toward choosing yune tools like resting, receiving, feeling, and observing. By using a combination of receptive and intention-based approaches, we can create a deeper level of balance within our practice and thus within ourselves.

Learning Adoga in Stages

Adoga is a complex practice. With all the possibilities we have discussed so far, we need a methodology for guiding our progression through learning the different practices of Adoga and then applying those practices throughout our lives once we are familiar with them.

Chapter Eight • The Methods of Adoga   151

We can summarize the progression of learning Adoga practices as follows:

1. Foundational Practices (See Chapter One)
   - Relax and Release
   - Grounding
   - Connecting to Heaven

2. Individual Practices on the Ado Tree (See Chapter Four)
   - Observation (Yunor 1.2)
   - Imagination (Kavek 2.1)
   - Feeling (Yunem 1.1)
   - Intention (Kavos 2.2)
   - Receiving (Yune 1)
   - Creating (Kav 2)

3. Practices of Rest (See Chapter Five)
   - Releasing Direct Intention and Immediate Goals (Kavos 2.2)
   - Releasing Imagination, Fixations, and Larger Goals (Kavek 2.1)
   - Releasing Observation and Inner Divisions (Yunor 1.2)
   - Releasing Foundational Energies (Yunem 1.1)
   - Releasing Intention (Kav 2)
   - Releasing Consciousness (Yune 1)

4. Methods of Adoga (See Chapter Eight)
    - Alignment
    - Symmetry
    - Flexible Intention
    - Fixed Intention

5. Expansions (See Chapter Nine)
    - In no particular order: Practicing Adoga in Day-to-Day Life, Discovery Progression, Practices on the Eight-Part Level of Division, the Mental Discovery System, Relational Practice

Thus far, we have made it through the four methods of Adoga on this progression. In the next chapter, we will progress to the expansions, which can be learned in any order.

Before moving on to the expansions, we will examine the process of a dedicated session of Adoga practice. In combination with the order of practices above, this will provide a framework for selecting which practices to learn and use.

The Process of a Dedicated Session

Adoga can be practiced in dedicated sessions and also throughout day-to-day activities.

I recommend using the relax and release practice to open a dedicated session of Adoga. If you want to deepen this relaxation phase, you can use a progression of releasing practices moving from kavos (2.2) to kavek (2.1) to yunor (1.2) to yunem (1.1) or, alternatively, from kav (2) to yune (1). I invite you to add the grounding practice and the connecting to heaven practice to this opening section. Lastly, you may want to clarify your intentions for the session in this section. You might decide to focus on the receptive methods or the intention-based methods, for example. You also might select a specific issue or practice to work on, if you are working within the intention-based methods. Another possibility is to remain open and refrain from making any specific intentions, following whatever feels most natural among the possibilities you are familiar with.

After the opening portion of the session, you can progress to using one of the four methods: alignment, symmetry, flexible intention, or fixed intention. Toward the end of your session, I recommend a closing practice similar to the opening practice. We can use a combination receptive practices, relaxing and releasing practices, or balancing practices like grounding and connecting to heaven to facilitate integration and recovery. You also might seek to clarify in your mind if you have any takeaways from the session, perhaps an intention you want to set in your life or something of particular importance you want to remember.

As you gain experience, the practices will become more powerful and the option for more transformative experiences will open up to you. These more transformative experiences will require more rest and integration to recover from. More transformative experiences also will produce more dramatic physical manifestations of release (PMRs).

To allow for maximal transformation and the vulnerability that such transformation requires, I recommend setting up an intentionally created environment for dedicated sessions. Such an environment should allow you to be alone or with others who have a good understanding of PMRs and the willingness to be around emotional-spiritual release.

If you find yourself surrounded by the release of others and you find yourself receiving energies you would rather not hold on to, you can use the practices of relaxation and release, grounding, and connecting to heaven to let go of what doesn't serve you and rebalance your energies.

Chapter Nine
Expansions

Practicing Adoga in Day-to-Day Life

Perhaps the most important addition to the fundamentals of the Adoga framework is the ability to bring Adoga practices into day-to-day activities where they can more directly influence your decisions, relationships, and contribution to society.

  The practice of bringing Adoga into day-to-day life is to cyclically bring your attention to the reception (yune 1) and creation (kav 2) of your state in moments where you have the space to do so. This looks like an ongoing awareness of what your state wants to communicate to you combined with an ongoing practice of creating states that can be used as resources.

  Bringing alignment method into this process, you can notice if certain activities or situations seem to call for specific states. For example, you might decide to cultivate curious excitement (kaves 2.1.1) or inspiration (kavel 2.1.2) while writing a piece of fiction or you might decide to cultivate a yunem feeling state to increase your empathy in a relationship or you might cultivate a state of yunoj power while working out.

Execution and Discovery

I call the progression from yune to kav the *execution progression*. I call the opposite progression, moving from kav to yune, the *discovery progression*. The execution progression is primary and foundational. The discovery progression is essentially a variation on the execution progression, based on many of the same fundamental truths. As described in Chapter One, we will still generally associate yune with beginnings and kav with endings.

We can see the logic of the execution progression in the order of the practices on the ado tree. The process begins in yunem with receptivity, which leads to greater awareness of your situation. In yunor, we obtain freedom from our situation, which enables us to change and chart a new path. In kavek, we discover what this new path looks like, and then, in kavos, we implement our vision. This progression outlines the natural movement from understanding to choosing a path and then implementing that path.

An example of a discovery progression would be a scientific study that collects many data points at the beginning of the process and then arrives at one, general conclusion at the end of the process. In contrast, we might see the execution progression in a scientific paper that explains the study's findings, beginning by stating the general conclusion of a study and then proceeding to examine a multiplicity of details, specific data, examples,

Chapter Nine • Expansions

and applications.

When progressions tend to emphasize the movement from multiplicity into unity, they tend to focus on learning or the creation of general principles – in a word, discovery. When progressions tend to emphasize the movement from unity into multiplicity, they tend to focus on application or implementation within the context of established general principles.

The execution progression is foundationally active within the discovery progression. Although the discovery progression begins with a multiplicity of data (kav) and then arrives at a general conclusion (yune), it still uses a generally-oriented receptivity (yune) to learn from that data at the beginning of the process, and it still uses a specifically-oriented expression (kav) to articulate the general conclusion of the discovery process. This is why I say that the execution process is primary and foundational.

Thus far, we have been working with Adoga in the standard, execution paradigm. In this section, we will examine Adoga in the discovery paradigm. Looking at the practices in the discovery paradigm, we can see a progression from kavos (2.2) to yunem (1.1), in which the flavor of each practice is changed to align with the goal of discovering more about yourself and the self-growth process. In this paradigm, the goal is less about the direct creation of an emotional-spiritual state and more about discovering information that is relevant to your emotional-spiritual world: what the patterns of your current state are compared to the possibilities, what your intention can do and how, and, lastly, how to use the self-growth process more powerfully.

In the discovery progression, kavos takes on the form of experimenting with your intention. While in an execution process, we can cultivate a clear sense of what we want to intend through kavek imagination, in the discovery process we begin using our intention without clear objectives for changing our state but rather with the goal of discovering more about the possibilities of intention. It is advisable to be gentle, careful, and observant in this process. You'll want to move your intention in a certain way… and see what happens. Change your input and take note of the output. This is the data gathering phase of a discovery process. See if you can expand your awareness of the possibility space of emotional-spiritual intention. What can you do with your emotional-spiritual intention?

With a sufficient amount of data gathered, we can start to use our imagination (kavek 2.1) to create new possibilities that might exist as extensions or variations on the experiences we encountered in the kavos practice. In this phase, we will want to imagine using our intention in different ways. We no longer need to be so gentle now because we are experimenting within the safety of our imagination rather than in manifested reality. This opens up potential for exploring extremes and the more radical limits of our awareness. Imagination produces an extrapolated addition to our data set. Our extrapolated data stand on less certain ground in comparison to our manifested (kavos 2.2) data, but this extrapolated addition is helpful in beginning to formulate an understanding of the patterns behind our data.

Progressing to yunor (1.2) entails observing your experience, now with the intention of seeing how the newly discovered possibilities of the earlier phases are operating within your state or, alternatively, how they are absent from your state.

Finally, the discovery process ends in yunem (1.1) with the intention to feel into our experience. Here, we not only *see* newly discovered processes operating within us, we *connect* with them and take them in through emotional-spiritual receiving. Energy previously hidden away in the shadows can now be felt and integrated into our body, emotions, mind, and awareness.

This process moves from the experimental gathering of data to a deep understanding and emotional reception of these data. We can summarize this practice in following four steps:

1. Experiment with your intention. (2.2)

2. Imagine different ways of using your intention that might challenge your awareness of the possibility space. (2.1)

3. Observe how intention is operating within your own current experience. (1.2)

4. Feel into and immersively connect with your experience of emotional-spiritual intention. (1.1)

Practices on the Eight-Part Level of Division

One exciting element of Adoga is that there are, literally, endless ado positions to explore. In tree language, we can theorize an infinite number of positions. Ados are possible in every level of division, whether it is the division into two, three, four, five, or seventy-three parts. The question is what do they all mean?

In this section, we will look at one additional possibility: practices on the eight-part level of division. I think that covering the practices in an eight-part division will be a useful expansion to our core framework in two regards. First, breaking down the practices into more detail can allow us to address issues in a more targeted, specific fashion, which can be helpful at times. Second, thinking of the practices as a sequence of eight may make it easier to make connections to the eight-part description of emotions and states I presented in Chapter Six. We will find that practices on the eight-part level of division are somewhat more difficult to name and describe succinctly.

To begin, let's consider how yunem feeling (1.1) could be broken down into component parts. In the context of practices, I think of the kav component of feeling – yunet (1.1.2) – as the intention to *receive the intensity and richness of life*. Here, we are feeling in an immersive way but with specific intention toward taking in the kav, full, or intense aspect of life. In contrast, the yune component of feeling – yunes (1.1.1) – is a more simplistic intention toward opening up to and feeling an experience. The interesting thing about yunes, however, is that we don't need to be able to take in the full extent of an experience – that's the job of yunet. And therefore, we can take on more challenging experiences. This more yune tool can reach farther into the shadows of emotional-spiritual depth, though the awareness we will receive back will be more dimly lit. We could call the yunes practice the intention toward *initial opening*. It feels like an intention to open up and turn into the truth of reality. In yunet, we are already somewhat aware of reality, and we now grow in our capacity to let its fullest nature flow through us. We strive not to turn away from any part of the truth, no matter how challenging.

In the yunor (1.2) area of practice, we have two more possibilities. The yune component of yunor – yunov 1.2.1 – I think is best understood as being an even more inward version of yunor. Here we are utterly focused on and immersed in the spaciousness of the observing or witness self. This is the area of consciousness where the world might seem to fall away against the vastness of inward consciousness. The practice of yunov (1.2.1), then, becomes focused on *becoming aware of the observing self*. It is more about finding this part of the self than it is about observing anything in particular. In contrast, the kav component of yunor – yunoj (1.2.2) – brings back a more worldly focus. This practice aims to bring the potential and wisdom of yunor to the world, our understanding of the world, our feelings about the world, and our observation of specific objects in the world. This is the area of consciousness where feelings of oneness with the world (not just internal oneness) may arise. The practice of yunoj, then, is about quieting the mind and *taking in the observing self's perspective on what is observed or experienced*. Yunoj practice is like holding an awareness of that spacious and free observing self while deeply observing different objects or experiences in our environment. From here, we can allow the sense of unity we feel within the observing self to encompass both ourselves and our environment at the same time, arriving at the oneness of both self and world. Feelings of appreciation, big-picture connectivity, and even awe arise from this practice, if done successfully.

We have already discussed variations of the kavek (2.1) practice, and these will align fairly well with kaves (2.1.1) and kavel (2.1.2). Kaves is associated with what we have been calling simple imagination practice, whereas kavel is complex imagination practice. Another take on this is that kavel is realistic imagination. In other words, in kavel we imagine things that we think might happen – things we want or don't want in the situations in our life, possibilities we are concerned with because they could happen. In contrast, kaves imaginations like basic shapes have little baring on real possibilities of manifestation. However, they are important to the inward aspect of imagination that ripples out into manifested effects. Kaves also includes ridiculous or absurd imaginations, if we are not concerned that they might occur in the manifested world. Kaves might include imaginations that could happen, but realism is not an important aspect of why we are imagining the vision. For example, we might imagine a peaceful beach, not because we are preparing to go to the beach but just because it has a positive effect on our state.

In contrast, kavel might look like imagining the different ways your upcoming interview or date could go, noticing the emotions those imaginations bring up for you, and working on them. Or the realism could be a bit further in the future. Perhaps you are imagining the best way that your life could turn out ten years from now or the worst way it could turn out ten years from now.

Kavel imagination is concerned with possibilities that might occur in manifestation. Kaves imagination is concerned with building awareness and an emotional-spiritual state to increase our potential for interacting with manifestation. To summarize all these traits, we can think of kaves practice as *potential-oriented imagination* and kavel practice as *manifestation-oriented imagination*.

The kavos (2.2) intending region of the tree breaks down into kavoj (2.2.1) and kavov (2.2.2). There is a similar potential and manifestation duality at work here as well. I like to think of kavoj as *cultivating intending potential*. To practice kavoj, find your intending self and notice the ability, the potential, the power present in this energy. Connect with this energy. Marvel at it. Grow your ability to channel it. Invite it into you. With this increased potential, you can move into kavov by *releasing this potential into the world with direction and intent.*

To summarize, the list below presents each of these practices associated with their corresponding ado names and tree language. I have also included associations to the basic descriptors of these ados as emotions or states. These associations will be helpful for using the practices on the eight-part level division in alignment method and symmetry method.

1.1.1
Yunes
Practice: Initial Opening
Emotion: Hurt-Love

1.1.2
Yunet
Practice: Receiving Intensity and Richness
Emotion: Hate-Joy

1.2.1
Yunov
Practice: Becoming Aware of the Observing Self
Emotion: Depression-Peace

1.2.2
Yunoj
Practice: Receiving the Observing Self's Perspective on the Observed
Emotion: Grief-Appreciation

2.1.1
Kaves
Practice: Potential-Oriented Imagination
Emotion: Fear-Excitement

2.1.2
Kavel
Practice: Manifestation-Oriented Imagination
Emotion: Attachment-Inspiration

2.2.1
Kavoj
Practice: Cultivating Intending Potential
Emotion: Anger-Power

2.2.2
Kavov
Practice: Releasing Intending Potential Into Manifestation
Emotion: Frustration-Satisfaction

A Mental Discovery System

In this section, I'll present a system of mental discovery. This practice uses different forms of journaling, sometimes oriented toward concrete thought and sometimes oriented toward intuition. The practices we have examined so far are directed toward emotional-spiritual end goals (though we have used many intellectual processes along the way).

In this section, we will have the opportunity to explore end goals in the mental realm.

This mental discovery system is a form of the discovery progression, which moves from kav to yune. We can think of this process in two parts: a kav practice of data gathering and stream of consciousness journaling, followed by a yune practice of discovering patterns and solidifying conclusions, principles, and understandings.

The kav practice is essentially the act of writing your thoughts (or some of them) as they occur. This involves watching your mind much like an observational meditation. As you watch, you simultaneously find ways to record your thoughts in your journal. For this practice, I encourage you not to dwell on creating an ideal representation or expression of your thoughts. Simply, write the first thing that comes to mind and keep writing. Don't edit. Stay with your mind in the present moment and try to write as continuously as possible. Ideally, you want to enter a state of flow. The result can be nonsensical and messy. The goal is to create a snapshot of your mind for your own self-growth process.

You can use what I call intuitive journaling in this process as a potential variation. To practice intuitive journaling, pose a question or statement to yourself, and then practice yune receiving, listening for your emotional-spiritual response to the question or statement. Then, record the prompt and the response in your journal. Repeat the process as many times as desired. This can be a useful practice for getting touch with your intuitive wisdom and revealing what topics you are carrying emotional-spiritual energy around.

Finally, you may find that in dedicated sessions of self-growth you have new ideas and insights that arise as your emotional-spiritual state goes through progressive changes. Consider keeping a journal next to you when you perform dedicated sessions of self-growth so that you can briefly record these thoughts.

Over time, your stream of consciousness journaling entries, intuitive journaling entries, and journaling entries from self-growth sessions will build up a growing data pool of information about your psychology. Once you have a few kav journal entries, you can move into the yune practice of discovering patterns and insights. In this practice, you go over old entries and look for common threads. What conclusions can you draw from your data?

As you begin to entertain conclusions, you can further the process by refining your conclusions so that they summarize the most amount of truth the most succinctly. We want to know not just what conclusions we can draw from the data but what conclusions are the most important. What conclusions are the most solid and dependable? What conclusions are the most encompassing?

What we need to do is combine, relate, and integrate the conclusions we have come to in the previous phases of the discovery process. Essentially, we ask, "What conclusions are implied by other conclusions?" We then can ask, "What conclusion implies the most number of other important conclusions?" The answer to this question is the foundation, the seat of causal influence.

In your journal, you can work through this process by writing out your most encompassing conclusions next to each other. Then you can attempt to combine the conclusions together, in ways that don't sacrifice too much of the original complexity and truth. You can keep combining until you are left with a set of principles, a collection of phrases, or perhaps even a single phrase or word.

Upon discovering an encompassing and essential principle, we will also want to spend some time figuring out how best to express this principle. Expressions of your principles should make sense to you, first and foremost. However, you also may want to consider how to express your conclusions to others.

Relational Adoga

Relational Adoga is the possibility of practicing Adoga in groups. Relational Adoga offers two roles participants can take on. I call these the role of center and the role of support. For the sake of brevity, we can call people who are acting in the center role *centers* and, likewise, call people who are acting in the support role *supports*.

Centers are the focus of attention in their groups. There can only be one center at a time within a single group, but there can be many supports. The total number of people in a group can be anywhere from two up to the

Chapter Nine • Expansions

point where the sense of group cohesiveness breaks down.

The center performs the practice of Adoga, just as they would in individual Adoga, except with the additional layer of reporting what is happening in their experience to the group. The center does not have to share anything they don't want to, but they are encouraged to share anything they do want to.

The support or supports must focus their attention primarily on the center. We can use some Adoga practices to do this but not others. Yunor and kavek both possess a kind of dualistic quality that makes the support function possible. In yunor, there is the duality between observer and observed. In kavek, there is the duality between imagined potential and manifestation. In both cases, we can take on an object of focus outside of ourselves. We can observe the external world in yunor, and we can imagine the external world in kavek. Yunem feeling and kavos intention cannot take on external objects of focus in the same way. (Consider directly feeling or intending the external world.)

As I see it, the support role is focused on observing (yunor 1.2) the center and imagining (kavek 2.1) the center's experience – empathizing, in other words. Supports may do a lot of listening to the center report their experience. They also may ask questions about the center's experience. They can develop understandings or imaginations of the center's experience and then inquire as to the accuracy of their ideas.

The process of centers sharing their experience

while supports listen and seek to understand creates a powerful effect whereby multiple people can share in a singular experience, bringing their hearts, minds, and spirits together. This enhances the center's growth experience and also creates (often unexpected) benefits for the supports. By listening to another's experience, the supports can expand their possibility space, bringing awareness to possibilities that they may not have experienced but now can learn from through another's life experience.

Conversation between the center and the supports is generally necessary to establish connection. However, there is a danger that conversation may overstimulate the mind. Thinking should probably be keep present yet minimalistic, to allow for a focus on emotional-spiritual states. The center should also stay focused on mostly reporting their experience in the present moment and emotional-spiritual domain.

The roles of center and support may be established at the beginning of a session and be maintained in a fixed manner throughout the duration of the session. Or these roles may be allowed to organically change throughout a session in a flexible manner.

Conclusion
Imagining the World Anew

To bring this journey to a close, I will take a moment to reflect on what self-growth could mean for you and for society. What can we all do to move forward? What is Adoga's place in the path ahead?

A Growing World

What would it be like if everyone had access to Adoga or an alternative that is just as effective and encompassing? What if it were the norm to be skilled at practices like yune receiving and kav creating as well as their components and variations? What if ado-based maps could help to guide people, businesses, and societies toward more inclusive and balanced viewpoints?

This is a world that is mostly incomprehensible right now. What if it became commonplace to occupy a well-developed state of consciousness? Aliveness, compassion, purpose, clarity of mind, peacefulness, the ability to focus, and the capacity to flexibly imagine new potentials – all available as resources. If problems arose, one could use a self-growth practice to find their way again. People would have the ability to *create their emotional-spiritual state*. If they wanted to be full of joy, it is just a practice away. If they wanted to feel ecstasy, they could. If they wanted to focus and have clarity of mind for working, they could. If they wanted to remain loving and connected in their relationship, they could.

Along with the creative expression of state, people would also receive the wisdom of the various states. People could have access to internal advisors – a part of the self that speaks for the lovingness of the heart, another part that speaks for the intelligence of the head, perhaps another part that speaks for the spirit or the primal wisdom within.

People would still be imperfect. People would still have problems. Perhaps if larger problems in the emotional-spiritual domain arose, there would be systems or protocols or ceremonies to deal with such occurrences. As certain problems become mostly resolved, new problems would appear, new challenges, the next domain. It is difficult to say what these problems might be, but the principle of infinite potential tells us they are coming. However, we can also be certain that those problems will be *better problems.*

Progress is possible. Perfection is not. But when we understand what progress and perfection really mean, it becomes apparent that progress is worth fighting for and perfection is *not* worth worrying about. A perfect world would be boring, if it existed. There would be nothing to do. A progressing world is exciting and engaging and, fortunately, this is the world that we are all challenged to participate in, to create and recreate.

Urgency and Peace

These are important ideas. When I first discovered the world of self-growth, I felt a profound sense of urgency and an internal recognition of the significance of what I was learning. When self-growth really begins to work and you begin to experience significant changes in your own state, it becomes exciting – really exciting. For me, self-growth even became an *obsession* at times. A sense of profound urgency is still with me today and, indeed, functions as a useful source of inspiration, but I have had to develop the capacity to balance that urgency with *peace*.

Peace comes from knowing that not everything that needs to be done can be done in one day. It comes from knowing that when it is time to rest, it is time to leave the worries of tomorrow for tomorrow. It also comes from knowing that you cannot force people to change, nor is it moral to do so. People need to grow. Yes. But that growth needs to take place of their own volition and because *they* understand the necessity of the growth, not because you do.

Where Do We Go From Here?

For the sake of our own sanity and our own emotional-spiritual states, we all must come our own place of balance, bringing peace to our sense of urgency. That being said, there are things that we all can do to work toward a better world, very important things. To begin with, we can work on our own self-growth. If we grow and develop ourselves, the externals in life naturally follow. Secondly, we can't force people to change, but we can be supportive, even actively supportive. We can share our passions. We can be there for people's struggles. We can help people, when they are open to receiving it. We can be good friends, partners, leaders, parents, siblings, and children.

Furthermore, the foundations of Adoga and other self-growth systems must be brought into the relational and external domains. This means coming together as a self-growth community. It means finding like-minded people and establishing structures and methods that make the task of coming together possible. It means harnessing the synergistic power of relationships and groups.

I invite you to incorporate Adoga into your contributions to the external world. Discover the states that optimize your performance in certain tasks. Apply ado maps to your field of expertise. Create enterprises that have a strong purpose and solid foundations in self-growth and philosophy. Create enterprises that take us in a direction worth going in and use methods that are don't compromise our values, emotions, and spirits to get there.

There is much to do. And much to lose, if Adoga and its friends in the self-growth community fail in their paramount tasks. Be bold and courageous. Never give up on your inspirations. And always remember to love yourself, your fellow beings of life, and the whole world.

Thank you for reading.

Appendix 1
A Map of the Ado Tree

Yune (1)
- Unity
- Generality
- Receptivity
- Inwardness
- Self
- Awareness
- Rest
- Causal Principles
- Potential
- Beginnings

Kav (2)
- Multiplicity
- Specificity
- Expression
- Outwardness
- World
- Intention
- Activity
- Manifestation
- Endings

Yunem (1.1)
- The Practice of Feeling
- The Release of Foundational Energies
- Unified, Immersive Experiences
- The Psychology of Essence and Identity
- The Choice Between Shame or Forgiveness

Yunor (1.2)
- The Practice of Observing
- The Release of Inner Divisions
- The Creation of Perspectives
- Experiences of the Formless Divine
- The Psychology of Freedom and Possibility

Kavek (2.1)
- The Practice of Imagining
- The Release of Imagination, Fixation, and Larger Goals
- Emotions that Relate to (Specific or External) Potentials
- The Psychology of Purpose and Clarity

Kavos (2.2)
- The Practice of Direct Intention Toward a State
- The Release of Direct Intention & Immediate Goals
- Emotions that Relate to Manifestation or End Results
- The Psychology of Focus and Resonance

Yunes (1.1.1)
- The Practice of Initial Opening
- Fundamental Needs
- Negative States:
    - Hurt
    - Shame
- Positive States:
    - Love
    - Forgiveness

Yunet (1.1.2)
- The Practice of Receiving Intensity and Richness
- A (Good or Bad) Attitude Applied Broadly to the External World
- Negative States:
    - Hate
    - Guilt
- Positive States:
    - Joy
    - Playfulness

Yunov (1.2.1)
- The Practice of Becoming Aware of the Observing Self
- The Witness
- Negative States:
    - Depression
    - Numbness
    - Apathy
    - Repression
- Positive States:
    - Peace
    - Spaciousness
    - Focus
    - Freedom
    - Stability
    - The Formless Divine

Yunoj (1.2.2)
- The Practice of Receiving the Observing Self's Perspective on the Observed
- Negative States:
    - Grief
    - Sadness
- Positive States:
    - Appreciation
    - Gratitude
    - Awe
    - Divine Complexity
    - Wisdom

Kaves (2.1.1)

- The Practice of Potential-Oriented Imagination
    - Simple Imagination Practice
    - Absurd Imaginations or Other Imaginations That Are Distantly Related to Manifestation
- Negative States:
    - Fear
    - Anxiety
- Positive States:
    - Excitement
    - Hope
    - Curiosity
    - Exploration

Kavel (2.1.2)

- The Practice of Manifestation-Oriented Imagination
    - Imagining What You Want
    - Imagining What You Don't Want
- Negative States:
    - Attachment
    - Obsession
    - Greed
    - Mania
- Positive States:
    - Inspiration
    - Passion
    - Purpose

Kavoj (2.2.1)
- The Practice of Cultivating Intending Potential
- Negative States:
  - Anger
  - Powerlessness
- Positive States:
  - Power
  - The Ability to Positively Affect Manifestation

Kavov (2.2.2)
- The Practice of Releasing Intending Potential Into Manifestation
- Negative States:
  - Frustration
  - Dissatisfaction
  - Feeling Deprived
- Positive States:
  - Satisfaction
  - Pleasure
  - Fulfillment
  - Happiness

Appendix 2
Yin, Yang, and the Elemental Archetypes

This appendix briefly touches on a complicated topic that I hope to write more about in the future.

I studied many systems of archetypes in the process of creating Adoga. Chief among them is the great and ancient concept of yin and yang, which initially occupied the place of yune and kav in the Adoga system. As Adoga developed, it became apparent that the historical meanings of yin and yang were deviating from the 1 and 2 positions in the Adoga system, and this created a need for new words.

The study of elemental systems was also important in Adoga's development. The *I Ching* is one such system from ancient China based on elements like earth, fire, and water. With incredible richness and detail the *I Ching* describes sixty-four elemental archetypes in a mathematical structure similar to Adoga. Though, the premise of the *I Ching* is remarkable similar to Adoga, the outcome is different. In fact, all elemental systems that I've encountered deviate strongly from Adoga, though also create a profound connection.

I think it would be worth describing one influential system of Western origin that comprises four elements: earth, water, fire, and air. (Note that there is also a five-element system of Eastern origin as well as the previously mentioned *I Ching*, which is based on eight elements that combine into sixty-four archetypes. Though there is overlap between these elemental systems, there are also important differences.) While referencing a physical phenomenon in the natural world, on a deeper level, each element refers to a metaphysical archetype. Earth is associated with stability, manifestation, wealth, abundance, balance, and nourishment; water with emotion, wisdom, absorption, purification, flexibility, and intuition; fire with transformation, passion, change, energy, and leadership; air with intelligence, the mind, communication, the complementary opposite of "earthy" manifestation, dreams, and imagination. Earth and water are yin elements, whereas fire and air are yang elements.

Though I wasn't aware of this at the time of Adoga's initial creation, the four elements align well with the four trees: fire with practices, earth with rest, water with emotions, and air with thoughts. We will find that the elements do not correlate with ados well at all. Rather, they represent a complementary yet opposite way of understanding archetypal wisdom. I do not see one perspective as superior to the other. Instead, they seem to create a fascinating synergy.

The four elements can help us to understand how yune and kav deviate from yin and yang. The element of earth perhaps reveals the difference between the two systems most clearly. Earth is a part of yin – this is more true in some spiritual systems than it is in others, but the general idea often holds true. However, the archetype of earth does not have a clear association to any ado. While its quality of stability is perhaps shared with yunor, its focus on manifestation opposes yunor. We can find other deviations between Adoga and the elements, but this is perhaps one of the most fundamental differences.

I feel it is helpful to mention all of this to clarify the associations and differences that exist between Adoga and other spiritual systems. Yin and yang sometimes align well with yune and kav, depending on context. And you may find associations between elemental systems and Adoga that work well. I encourage the study of all these perspectives.

Let us do our best to use the terms of each archetypal system with clarity. Referencing a specific spiritual system or teacher may be helpful in creating important context. In this way, we can keep the definitions of these many archetypes clear and meaningful.

Acknowledgments

Justin Taylor, my brother and dear friend, was my creative partner during the formation of the initial versions of Adoga. Together, we philosophized, intuited, tested, challenged, learned, studied, and practiced self-growth. The first versions of symmetry method were created through my collaboration with Justin. As I recall, it was Justin who came up with the acronym *ado*. These are just a few of the innovations that Justin helped to create. The beginnings of Adoga were a magical and profound time in my life. I deeply cherish the transformative co-creation and co-exploration that I experienced with Justin during this time.

Leonard Rosenbaum did the copyediting, proofreading, and index for this book. I want to thank Leonard for all his hard work. I appreciate his clear communication and expertise. He patiently and humbly pursued a deep understanding of my writing. Leonard greatly helped me to create a more succinct, clear, and effective book.

Sarah Taub gave me wonderful feedback and encouragement toward the end of my creative process with this book. Sarah helped me redesign tree language. She also helped me to clarify my explanation of the principle of infinite potential. Thank you, Sarah. Your enthusiasm and insight mean a lot to me.

Indigo Dawn helped me shape the expression of my ideas. They gave me insights about the balance between simplicity and oversimplification in teaching. They also gave me new associations to the ados, such as the association of hope to kaves. Indigo also tested many of the practices of Adoga with me, which gave me valuable data about how the practices operate in different people. Thank you so much for your incredibly constructive collaboration and feedback.

Roving illustrated the cover for this book and also helped me clarify my writing. I am amazed at Roving's creativity, artistry, and perception. I am deeply grateful to have Roving's work included in this project. Thank you so much for your contributions.

Sam Elmore gifted me with connecting enthusiasm and several pieces of valuable feedback. In particular, I want to thank Sam for helping me to differentiate listening to dysfunctional emotions from believing in the voice of dysfunctional emotions or buying into their stories.

Dahlia taught me about the elemental archetypes and grounding. They sparked an important investigation into the meaning and history of yin and yang. Dahlia also helped me develop the names of the ados. Thank you.

Brad Wasserman taught me about the practices of acceptance and letting go, which helped inform my creation of yune practices. Brad also taught me about subtle energy and creative intentions. Another teaching that Brad shared with me gave me insight into how anger was connected to deprivation. All of these teachings have influenced this book. Thank you.

Jaime Zoltick curiously and enthusiastically tested the practice of Adoga, giving me valuable insight into how the practices operate in different people. Thank you.

Lynn Haas, my loving mom, helped me edit this book. She also helps to create the Project Ado website, where you can access articles and other content related to Adoga. Thank you.

Myla Green introduced me to *Re-Evaluation Counseling* (RC). My experience with RC and with my teacher *Liz Araujo* taught me the healing power of emotional expression. The concept of PMRs in this book is inspired by the notion of "discharge" in RC.

Along with RC, *The Integral Center* in Boulder, CO and the larger community of *circling* practitioners around the world helped to inspire the concept of relational Adoga.

The Cambridge Insight Meditation Center (CIMC) helped me learn *Vipassana Meditation*, which influenced of my understanding of several practices, especially the yunor practice. I, also, first learned *metta meditation* at CIMC, which helped inspire the practice of *creating love and gratitude* in Chapter One.

Though I have my critiques of every author I studied while researching for this book, each contributed something unique to my understanding.

The books of *David Hawkins* were influential in my understanding of archetypes and my initial formation of the concepts for the ados. These works also helped me to develop my intuition. The works of *Ken Wilber* inspired some of my ideas about our use of language in spiritual community. Wilber's work also contributed my understanding of archetypes. The books and videos of *Eckhart Tolle* gave me much of my initial understanding of oneness and surrounding concepts in Eastern Philosophy. The work of *Donna Eden* helped inspire my understanding of subtle energy. *Jeffrey Chappell's Answers From Silence* helped inspire the practice of intuitive journaling. The works of *Steve Pavlina, Tony Robbins, Joe Dispenza,* and *Napoleon Hill* helped inspire my understanding of imagination (kavek) and intention-based (kavos) practices.

Thank you all who have contributed to the creation of this book. Though it would be impossible to name all of you, I feel you all in my heart.

Bibliography

Amara, HeatherAsh. *Warrior Heart Practice*. Griffin, 2020.

Angeles, Ly De. *Witchcraft: Theory and Practice*. Llewellyn Publications, 2000.

Chappell, Jeffrey. *Answers From Silence*. Book Surge, 2009.

"Creating Abundance." *YouTube*, uploaded by Steve Pavlina, 5 Nov. 2009, www.youtube.com/watch?v=Ad1DhUdtcFs.

Dispenza, Joe. *Becoming Supernatural*. Hay House, 2017.

Eden, Donna, and David Feinstein. *Energy Medicine*. Penguin Group, 1998.

Stone, Aine. "Elements & Correspondences." *The New Pagan*, thenewpagan.wordpress.com/elements-correspondences/. Accessed 11 Feb. 2020.

"The Gnostic Book of Changes." *James DeKorne*, www.jamesdekorne.com/GBCh/GBCh.htm.

Hawkins, David R. *Power vs. Force*. Hay House, 1995.

Hill, Napoleon. *Think and Grow Rich*. TarcherPerigee, 2005.

Holy Bible: From the Ancient Eastern Text: George M. Lamsa's Translation From the Aramaic of the Peshitta. Harper & Row, 1985.

Koestler, Arthur. *The Ghost in the Machine*. Hutchinson, 1967.

Laloux, Frederic. *Reinventing Organizations*. Nelson Parker, 2014.

Pirsig, Robert. *Zen and the Art of Motorcycle Maintenance*. Quill, 1979.

"Receive." *YouTube*, www.youtube.com/watch?v=7i-MGxVkhIk.

Regardie, Israel. *The Middle Pillar*. Llewellyn Publications, 1998.

Robbins, Tony. *Awaken the Giant Within*. Simon & Schuster, 1993.

Tolle, Eckhart. *The Power of Now*. New World Library, 1999.

Tzu, Lao. *Tao Te Ching*. Translated by Richard Wilhelm, Arkana, 1990.

Wallis, Christopher. "The Real Story on the Chakras." *Hareesh*, 5 Feb. 2016, hareesh.org/blog/2016/2/5/the-real-story-on-the-chakras.

Wilber, Ken. *Sex, Ecology, Spirituality* (2nd ed.). Shambhala, 2000.

Wilber, Ken. *The Religion of Tomorrow*. Shambhala, 2017.

Index

adaptive thinking, 106, 124
ado (archetypal division of oneness)
    archetypes and, 54, 182–83
    defined, 54
    positive and negative polarities of each, 98, 101
    the world of the, 54–56
ado tree(s), 62–63, 64f, 67f, 93, 94f, 100f, 109, 115f, 139f, 140, 156
    map of the, 175–80
    symmetries in visual depictions of, 141
Adoga (archetypal divisions of oneness growth activity)
    in day-to-day life, practicing, 91, 152, 155
    definitions, 8, 54
    focus of, 8
    four methods of, 152, 153 (*see also specific methods*)
    and the future, 173–74
    goal of, 9–10
    overview and nature of, 8–10, 13–15, 18, 66
    what it offers, 8–10
    See also specific topics
Adoga sessions, dedicated
    the process of a, 152–54
    See also self-growth sessions, dedicated
aligning practice
    with potential energy, 146–48
    with state, 136–38, 140
alignment, 128
    of internal and external, 121, 131
alignment method, 137–38, 139f, 140–44, 150, 155
    flexible intention method and, 149
    nature of, 148
    overview, 137
    potential energy and, 147
    resistance and, 149
    symmetry method and, 141–43, 148–50
    ways of approaching the, 147–48
    yune and, 148
    See also aligning practice
allowing, 76–79

anger, 112, 141, 142
    kavoj and, 112, 134, 146 (*see also* kavoj)
    power, powerlessness, and, 112, 134, 146
appreciation, 31, 71, 79, 109, 129–30, 133, 140, 162. *See also* yunoj
archetypal division of oneness. *See* ado
archetypal divisions of oneness growth activity. *See* Adoga
archetypes
    ado and, 54, 182–83
    Adoga and, 8, 54, 181–82
    defined, 54
    elemental, 181–83
assumptions, questioning, 124, 125
attachment, 88
    kavel and, 111, 133–34, 146
    observing self and, 76, 77, 106–7
    possibilities and, 133, 146
    yunor and, 107, 133

bad attitude, 102–3. *See also* negativity
balance, 19, 27, 92, 119–21, 142, 150, 173
    of positive and negative, 86
    principle of, 144–45
    yunor and, 133 (*see also* yunor)
barriers, 36, 73–74, 83, 87, 107. *See also* resistance
brain, 23
breath, 25, 33
    observing one's, 29, 75, 76, 85
    pulsating, 33
    subtle energies and, 25

causal principles, 27
    yune and, 19–20
center, role of, 168, 170
centers (people acting in the center role), 168–70
centers of subtle energy, 22–25, 29, 90
    defined, 23
    focusing on, 29, 30, 68, 75, 79, 90
    observing, 28–30
chakras. *See* centers of subtle energy
characteristics, defining, 55–56
clarity, 73. *See also* purpose and clarity
contrast, 41, 48–49, 124
    definitions as relying on, 41–42, 48, 49, 90
    holans and, 48, 49, 55, 75

Index 193

    lack of, 41, 49, 123–24
    oneness and, 49, 55
    thinking and, 41, 42, 45, 48, 80
creating, 73
creative thinking, 124
creativity, 28, 109, 128, 149
crying, 33–35

Dao, 39, 50. *See also* yin and yang
Dao De Jing, 39, 50
defining characteristics, 55–56
definition(s)
    nature of, 41–42, 45–49
    as relying on contrast, 41–42, 48, 49, 90
dense energy, 21, 22
depression, 141, 145
    inspiration and, 141, 145
    possibility space and, 123, 145
    repression and, 106, 123
    yunov and, 106, 133, 145, 147
discovery progression (from kav to yune), 153, 156–58, 166, 167
discovery system. *See* mental discovery system
division of oneness, 13, 18, 54–55, 62
    defined, 54
    See also ado; Adoga
duality, 169. *See also* non-duality; opposites

earth, 182–83
    connecting to, 27
ecstasy. *See* joy
Eden, Donna, 21–22
elemental archetypes. *See* archetypes
elements, four, 181, 182
emotional satisfaction, 9, 28. *See also* satisfaction
emotional-spiritual expression, a societal shift surrounding, 36–37
emotional-spiritual state(s), 102
    Adoga and improvement of one's, 8
    kav and, 30, 73, 74, 102, 112
    nature of, 8
emotions
    eight pairs of, 138, 139f, 140
    essential, 102
    listening to, 28

positive, 24, 31, 87, 91, 92, 101, 117
    See also negative emotions; tree of emotions
empathy, 122, 155
"ends justify the means" thinking, 111
energy
    definitions, 47
    dense, 21, 22
    form, holan, and, 45–48
    nature of, 21
    See also centers of subtle energy
energy body, 22
essence, 102, 103, 133
    acceptance of a person's, 10
    yunem and, 132–34
essence and identity, 116, 132–33. *See also* yunem
essence and identity psychology, 128, 142
essential aspects of things, 47
essential level and essential nature of things, 116
essential needs, 102
excitement, 110, 142
    kaves and, 110, 133, 146, 147, 155 (*see also* kaves)
execution progression (from yune to kav), 89–90, 156, 157

fear, 110
    imagination and, 110, 133, 136
    kavek and, 136
    kaves and, 110, 133, 146
Fia, 127
fish in water, 44, 123
    fish unaware that it's in water, 40, 41
fixed intention method, 149–50
flexible intention method, 149, 150
flexible thinking, 124
focus, 27–30, 101, 132, 134, 142, 169
    imagination and, 80, 85
    intention(s) and, 37, 70, 73, 75, 134, 144, 149, 150
    kavek and, 89, 90, 96
    kavos and, 128, 169 (*see also* kavos)
    and multiplicity of states and possibilities, 73, 89–90
    negative, 109, 128, 131
    objects of, 29, 30, 75, 102, 103, 132, 169
    positive, 107–9, 128, 131
    releasing, 95, 96
    repression and, 105, 106

Index . 195

yune, 70, 78, 95, 103
    yunem and, 89
    yunes and, 102, 103
    yunet and, 102–3
    yunoj and, 109
    yunor and, 75, 78, 104, 108
    yunov and, 107–8
    See also centers of subtle energy: focusing on
forgiveness, 10, 11, 117, 122
    benefits of, 118, 120–22, 146
    nature of, 117–18
    unconditional, 117, 121
    yunem and, 117, 121, 133
form, 45–47
    defined, 45
    definition and, 45–47
    energy and, 47
    holan and, 46, 47
    use of the term, 45, 47
formlessness, 95–96
    defined, 45–46
four trees of Adoga, 15–16, 68, 132–34
    and the four elements, 182
    as holarchies, 66
    as maps, 66
    See also specific topics; specific trees
free thinking, 124
freedom, 88
    observation and, 77, 105–7
    perspective and, 108, 124
    possibility space and, 123, 133, 134, 142 (*see also under* yunor)
    psychology of, 133, 142
    yunoj experience of, 146
    yunor and, 77, 88, 107, 123, 133, 134, 156 (*see also under* yunor)
frustration, 113, 134, 146
fulfillment, 113, 120, 141

God. *See* oneness
gratitude, 109
    creating, 31
    See also appreciation
grief, 109, 133, 142, 145. *See also* yunoj
grounding, 27

growth needs, 173. *See also* self-growth
guilt, 103, 104, 116
gut center, 23–24. *See also* centers of subtle energy

habits
    perspectives and, 14, 77, 123
    questioning, 124, 126
    transcending, 14, 77, 123
hate, 102–4, 116, 119, 121, 122, 131, 133
    love and, 10, 116, 133
    negative judgments and, 117, 133
    yunem and, 116, 117
    yunet and, 102–3, 145
head center, 24–25
    observation of, 44
    See also centers of subtle energy
heart, yunem and the, 79, 104
heart center, 22–25, 29, 75, 79
"heart space" vs. "head space," 110
heart warmth, 104
heartache, 104
heaven, connecting to, 28, 153, 154
holans, 75
    balancing, 92
    contrast and, 48, 49, 55, 75
    definition and nature of, 46, 47, 49
    form, energy, and, 47–49
    kav, 74, 102, 142
    oneness and, 49, 55
    principle of infinite potential and, 48–49
    biggest possible, 48, 49
    symmetrical, 142
    tree language and, 58, 61–62
    on the tree of emotions, 101, 147
    yune, 74, 75, 102, 142
honesty and truthfulness, 128, 129, 142
hurt, 102–4, 110, 118, 121, 133, 141. *See also* crying

I Ching, 181
identity. *See* essence and identity
imagination, 158–59
    complex, 84, 90, 162
    fear and, 110, 133, 136
    kav and, 80, 85, 88–89

Index

    kavel and, 109, 162, 163
    kaves and, 109, 110, 143, 162–63
    and possibilities, 133, 158–59, 162, 163
    possibility space and, 86, 145
    simple, 83–85, 90, 143, 162
imagining, 30, 81, 84, 91, 147
    intention and, 86, 88–89, 147
    kavel and, 163
    what we don't want, 81, 86
    See also kavek
infinity, 55, 108
initial opening, 161
inspiration, 11
    depression and, 141, 145
    kavek and, 136–37
    kavel and, 111, 134, 145, 155 (*see also* kavel)
    urgency and, 173
intention
    focus and, 37, 70, 73, 75, 134, 144, 149, 150
    imagining and, 86, 88–89, 147
    kav and, 75, 85, 88–89, 95, 112, 148, 160
    possibilities and, 153, 157–58
    possibility space and, 95, 149, 158, 159
    resistance and, 70–71, 73, 86–88, 149, 150
    See also kavos
intentions, 68–69
    relaxing, 70, 95, 96, 147

Jesus, 116
journaling, 165–68
    intuitive, 166–67
joy, 141, 142, 171
    yunet and, 103, 133, 146
    See also emotions: positive
judgment
    belief in the permanence of a, 116–17
    forgiveness and, 117–18, 133
    negative, 11, 117, 133
    positive, 133

kav, 74, 175
    defined, 18
    emotional-spiritual states and, 30, 73, 74, 102, 112
    guilt and, 103

imagination and, 80, 85, 88–89
intention and, 75, 85, 88–89, 95, 112, 148, 160
journaling and, 166, 167
kavek and, 80, 88, 91, 126
kaves and, 109, 110, 147
kavoj and, 112, 147
kavos and, 88, 91, 112
kavov and, 113
multiplicity and, 18–20, 73, 157
nature of, 18–20, 20t, 73, 108
and the observed self, 108
thinking and, 43
yunor and, 75, 108, 161
See also yune and kav
kav creating, 73–74, 88–89
kav half of the tree of emotions, 109, 110
kav holans and, 74, 102, 142
kav practice, 30, 73–74, 89–90, 166
kavek, 80–86, 156, 158, 176
    dualistic quality, 169
    focus and, 89, 90, 96
    kav and, 80, 88, 91, 126
    kavel and, 109, 133, 162
    kaves and, 109, 133, 162
    kavoj and, 112
    kavos and, 86–91, 96, 156, 158
    possibilities and, 81, 82, 125, 133, 158
    purpose, clarity, and, 125–27
    relation to other ados, 89–90, 153
    yunor and, 97, 153, 169
    See also purpose and clarity
kavek imaginative state, 96
kavek practice, 80, 85, 86, 127, 136–37
    variations of, 83–84
kavek processes, 136
kavek states, positive and negative, 110, 111, 136
kavek thinking, 125, 126
kavel, 133–34, 145, 165, 179
    attachment and, 111, 133–34, 146
    imagination and, 109, 162, 163
    inspiration and, 111, 134, 145, 155
    kavek and, 109, 133, 162
    kaves and, 109–11, 162
    nature of, 111

Index   199

    possibilities and, 145, 146, 162, 163
    purpose and, 111
    yunov and, 141, 146
kavel states, positive and negative, 111
kaves, 165, 179
    fear, anxiety, and, 110, 133, 143, 146
    imagination and, 109, 110, 143, 162–63
    kav and, 109, 110, 147
    kavek and, 109, 133, 162
    kavel and, 109–11, 162
    overview and nature of, 109–11
    positive and negative polarities of, 110
    possibilities and, 110–11, 133, 146
    yunoj and, 141, 145–46
kavoj, 112, 147, 163, 165, 180
    anger and, 112, 134, 146
    kavos and, 134, 148, 163
    nature of, 163
    positive and negative aspects of, 112, 148, 180
    power and, 112, 134, 145–47, 180
    yunet and, 141, 145, 146
kavos, 87–90, 127–32, 134, 158, 163, 176
    defined, 86
    focus and, 128, 169
    kav and, 88, 91, 112
    kavek and, 86–91, 96, 156, 158
    kavoj and, 134, 148, 163
    nature of, 86–87, 96
    relation to other ados, 86, 88–90, 153, 157
    yunem and, 157, 169
kavov, 180
    fulfillment of, 141, 145
    positive and negative polarities of, 113
    satisfaction and, 113, 134, 141, 145
    yunes and, 113, 141, 146
known oneness, 55
    See also oneness
Koestler, Arthur, 46

Laloux, Frederic, 23
language. *See* words
laughing, 33, 36, 38
limiting thinking, 124
listening, 28

receptivity and, 28–29
long- and short-term strategies, balance between, 12, 13
love, 10, 11, 121, 122
    creating, 30, 31
    hate and, 10, 116, 133
    yunes and, 102, 103

malevolence, 117–19, 122
manifestation(s), 80–81. *See also* imagining
mental discovery system, 165–68
mind. *See* head center
multiplicity, 73
    kav and, 18–20, 73, 157
    unity, oneness, and, 13, 18, 19, 156–57
    yune and, 19, 20, 70, 157

needs and desires, 12, 13, 102, 103, 113, 141, 145, 173
negative emotional-spiritual states, 34, 35, 104, 120, 121, 136, 141, 177–80
negative emotions, 24, 92, 101, 104, 117, 141
negative focus, 109, 128, 131
negative judgments, 11, 117, 133
negative yunet, 102–4
negativity, 119, 128, 134. *See also* bad attitude
non-duality, 43, 45, 49. *See also* duality; oneness

observation, focused, 105, 169. *See also* focus
observing
    the centers and the breath, 28–30 (*see also* breath: observing one's)
    division/duality between observer and observed, 77, 78, 80, 108, 169
    yunor and, 75–78, 80, 88, 97, 104, 107, 108, 133, 134, 143, 169
    See also yunor
observing self, 76–77, 97, 106–7, 143
    attachment and, 76, 77, 106–7
    and freedom, 77, 106–7
    vs. observed experience, 77, 80
    oneness, observed experience, and, 76–77, 106, 108
    yune and, 76, 78, 83, 108, 150
    yunoj and, 104, 162
    yunov and, 104, 161 (*see also* yunov)
    See also observing; yunoj; yunor observing
oneness, 43–45, 162

Adoga and, 13–14
contrast and, 49, 55
defining, 49–50, 55
division of, 13, 18, 54–55, 62 (*see also* ado; Adoga)
experiencing a sense of, 43–45, 49–50
holans and, 49, 55
journey from many to one and from one back to many, 13–15
known, 55–56
multiplicity and, 13, 18, 19, 156–57
nature of, 50
observing self, observed experience, and, 76–77, 106, 108
practices for creating states of, 43–44
premise of, 13–14
and the self, 13
yune and, 89, 106, 108
yunoj and, 109
See also division of oneness; known oneness

opening
initial, 161
yunem feeling practice and, 78
opposites, 41–42. *See also* duality

pain. *See* hurt
passion, 111
peace, 173
urgency and, 173
yunov and, 133, 146, 147 (*see also* yunov)
See also positive emotions
perspective, 124, 162
and freedom, 108, 124
observational process and, 123–24
purpose and, 126
seeing life from another's, 122
sense of, 77, 105, 108, 109, 134, 140
perspectives, 123–24, 162
altering/transcending our, 73, 77
encompassing, 14
and habits, 14, 77, 123
oneness and, 13–14
philosophy and spirituality, meeting of, 49
physical manifestations of release (PMRs), 33–36, 38, 154
in Adoga, 37
nature of, 33, 34, 37

overview, 33
secondary, 38
pleasure, 8, 113
positive emotional-spiritual states, 8–9, 91, 104, 120, 121, 136, 141, 143, 163, 177–80
positive emotions, 31, 92, 101, 104, 117, 128, 140, 141
positive energies, 30
positive focus, 107–9, 128, 131
positive judgments, 133
possibilities, 20, 24–25, 133
    attachment and, 133, 146
    imagination and, 133, 158–59, 162, 163
    intention and, 153, 157–58
    kavek and, 81, 82, 125, 133, 158
    kavel and, 145, 146, 162, 163
    kaves and, 110–11, 133, 146
    manifestation and, 81, 162, 163
    receptivity vs. expression and, 18–19
    yunoj and, 133, 145–46
    yunor, freedom, and, 123–25, 133
    yunov and, 133, 145, 146
    See also under focus
possibility space, 90, 93, 159
    defined, 81
    depression and, 123, 145
    expanding awareness, knowledge, and understanding of the, 81, 82, 86, 125, 142, 145, 158, 170
    freedom and, 123, 133, 134, 142
    imagination and, 86, 145
    intention and, 95, 149, 158, 159
    kavek and, 81, 82, 125 (*see also under* kavek)
    kaves and, 110–11 (*see also under* kaves)
    limitations, 83, 85, 123
    and the progression from yune to kav, 89–90
    resistances and, 83, 85
    yunor and, 125, 134
power, 106, 112, 134
    anger and, 112, 134, 146
    kavoj and, 112, 134, 145–47, 180
powerlessness, 112, 146
principle of infinite potential, 51–54
    defined, 51
    holans and the, 48–49
    problems and the, 172

Index

purpose and clarity, 125–27
purpose and clarity psychology, 142

questioning habits and assumptions, 124–26

"Receive" (Fia), 127
receiving, 70–72, 119, 120, 130, 154, 160
    divided and undivided, 77
    emotional-spiritual, 130, 159
    intention and, 69, 70
    and releasing, 29, 154
    yune practice and, 69–70, 83, 86, 166 (*see also* yune receiving)
    yunem and, 78, 133
receptive vs. intention-based methods/approaches, 148, 150, 153.
        See also receptivity/reception: vs. expression
receptivity/reception, 18–20, 25, 29, 90
    Adoga and, 148, 150, 155
    equality between action and, 119
    vs. expression, 18–19, 90, 157 (*see also* receptive vs. intention-based methods/approaches)
    listening and, 28–29
    nature of, 19
    yune and, 18, 19, 29, 69, 70, 148, 155, 157 (*see also* yune receiving)
    yunem and, 156
relational Adoga, 168–70
    roles participants can take on in, 168
relax and release practice, 26–27, 152–54. *See also under* resistance; yunem
relaxation, 79, 95–97. *See also* resistance: relaxing/releasing
relaxing intentions, 70, 95, 96, 147
release
    subtle energy and, 26–27, 31
    See also physical manifestations of release; relax and release practice
releasing
    receiving and, 29, 154
    See also under repression; resistance
releasing focus, 95, 96
repression, 107
    defined, 105
    depression and, 106, 123
    focus and, 105, 106
    nature of, 105–6

releasing/healing, 71, 72, 79, 106
resistance and, 71, 105, 107
yunov and, 106
resistance, 79, 83, 85–86, 107–8, 150
    definition and nature of, 70–71, 107
    discovering, 107, 130
    experiencing, 73, 74
    intention and, 70–71, 73, 86–88, 149, 150
    kav and, 74
    negative yunov and, 107
    possibility space and, 83, 85
    relaxing/releasing, 71, 74, 87, 97, 107, 130 (*see also* relaxation)
    repression and, 71, 105, 107
    yune practices and, 74, 83, 85–87
    See also barriers
resonance, 128
    defined, 128
    between physical and nonphysical domains, 129
    principle of, 129
resonance frequency, natural, 128
rest, 92–93, 94f, 95–96, 140
    balancing activity and, 19, 92, 111, 144–45
    intention and, 19, 92
    practices of, 151
    yune and, 19, 140, 144–45

sadness. *See* crying; hurt; yunoj
satisfaction
    kavov and, 113, 134, 141, 145
    listening to emotions and, 28
    nature of, 113, 134
science
    Adoga, spirituality, and, 14–15
    subtle energy and, 22, 23
    Tesla on, 2
self-acceptance, 10, 11, 14. *See also* forgiveness; judgment
self-growth, 10, 173
    becoming an obsession/urgency, 173
    defined, 10
    importance, 11–13
    nature of, 11–13, 71
    self-love and, 10
    See also Adoga
self-growth practices, foundational, 25. *See also specific practices*

self-growth sessions, dedicated, 91–93, 167. *See also* Adoga
        sessions, dedicated
self-love, 10. *See also* forgiveness; judgment
shame, 119, 121–22
    guilt and, 103, 104
    letting go of, 10
    listening to our, 121–22
    nature of, 103–4, 116
    negative judgments and, 11, 117, 133
    negative yumen and, 117, 118
short- and long-term strategies, balance between, 12, 13
sighing, 33–34, 36, 38
simplicity, 25, 76, 84, 133. *See also* imagination: simple
spirit. *See* oneness
spiritual journey, many to one, 15. *See also* oneness
spirituality, journey of one to many, 15
spirituality and philosophy, meeting of, 49
subtle energy
    definition and nature of, 21
    vs. dense energy, 21
    Donna Eden on, 21–22
    names for, in various spiritual traditions, 21–22
    overview, 21–25
    release and, 26–27, 31
    terms for, 21–22
    See also centers of subtle energy
suffering, 120, 131
support, role of, 168–70
supports (people acting in support role), 168–70
symmetrical cycles of growth, 144–46
symmetrical practice, 143–44
symmetrical relationships, 141–43. *See also* symmetry method
symmetry
    meaning of, 142
    patterns and principles behind the concept of, 144–46
symmetry method, 148–50
    alignment method and, 141–43, 148–50
    and mysterious relationships of symmetry, 140–44
    performing the, 142–43

Tao Te Ching. *See Dao De Jing*
thing, 45
thinking, 40, 124
    contrast and, 41, 42, 45, 48, 80

defined, 40, 41, 43, 48
 kav and, 43
 oneness and, 43, 54
 origin of, 54
thought
 defining, 40, 41
 See also thinking
thoughts, nature of, 40–43
tree, defined, 46
tree language, 58, 61–63, 66, 160
 examples of trees labeled in, 58–59, 60f, 61, 64
 holans and, 58, 61–62
 nature of, 58
tree of emotions, 98–99, 100f, 137, 145, 147
 far-left side of the, 145
 holans on, 101, 147
 kav half of the, 109, 110
 right-most area of the, 112–13 (*see also* kavov)
 See also specific topics
tree of practices, 66, 67f, 68, 74
 kav half of the, 80
 middle of the, 89
 See also specific topics
tree of rest, 92–93, 94f, 133, 134. *See also* rest; *specific topics*
tree of thoughts, 115f, 132, 137, 142. *See also specific topics*
trees, ado. *See* ado tree(s)
trees of Adoga. *See* four trees of Adoga
trees of thoughts, 115f
truthfulness and honesty, 128, 129, 142

unification, 18
unified states, 50, 97
unity. *See* oneness
urgency, sense of, 173

Wallis, Christopher, 22
words, new, 56–58

yin and yang, 181–83
yune, 175
 alignment method and, 148
 focus and, 70, 78, 95
 multiplicity and, 19, 20, 70, 157
 nature of, 18–20, 20t

and the observing self, 76, 78, 83, 108, 150
oneness and, 89, 106, 108
resistance and, 74, 83, 85–87
rest and, 19, 140, 144–45
yunem and, 77, 78, 88, 91
yunes and, 160–61
yunor and, 75, 78, 88, 91, 108
See also specific topics
yune and kav, 55, 75, 77, 140, 142, 160–61
    balance and, 144–45
    cycles between, 113
    the duality of, 18–20, 20t
    holans and, 74, 102, 142
    potential energy and, 146, 147
    (discovery) progression from kav to yune, 153, 156, 157, 166, 167
    (execution) progression from yune to kav, 89–90, 156, 157
    resistances and, 74
    spectrum from yune to kav, 98, 113
    trees and, 68
    yin and yang and, 181–83
    yune receiving and kav creating, 88, 155, 171
    yunov and, 106
yune receiving, 70, 72–75, 77, 78, 83, 88, 155, 171. *See also* receiving; receptivity/reception: yune and
yunem, 156, 176
    and division between observing self and observed experience, 77, 78, 80
    essence and, 132–34
    experience and, 78, 79, 88, 134, 159–61
    forgiveness and, 117, 121, 133
    and the heart, 79, 104
    honesty, truthfulness, and, 122, 128, 129
    kav and, 108, 160
    negative, 116–18
    overview and nature of, 89, 132–34
    positive, 117–19, 121, 122
    questions of, 116
    receiving, receptivity, and, 78, 133, 156
    relation to other ados, 86, 88–90, 153, 157
    relaxing/releasing, 79, 97
    thinking of, 116
    yune and, 77, 78, 88, 91
    yunes and, 102, 160–61

        yunet and, 102, 160
        yunor and, 78, 80, 89, 91, 107, 108, 140, 153
    yunem feeling(s), 78–80, 83, 86, 88, 102, 104, 133, 140, 155, 159,
            169
        components, 160–61
        opening and, 78
    yunem psychology, 128, 130
    yunes, 133, 177
        focus and, 102, 103
        kavov and, 113, 141, 146
        nature of, 113, 161
        needs, wants, and, 113, 145
        negative, 102, 103, 143
        positive, 103
        yune and, 160–61
        yunem and, 102, 160–61
        yunet and, 102, 161
    yunet, 133, 145, 160, 161, 177
        essence and, 102
        joy and, 103, 133, 146
        kavoj and, 141, 145, 146
        nature of, 103
        negative, 102–4 (*see also* hate)
        positive, 103 (*see also* joy)
        yunem and, 102, 160
        yunes and, 102, 161
    yunoj, 108, 164, 178
        grief, sadness, and, 109, 133, 145–46
        kaves and, 141, 145–46
        nature of, 109
        observing and, 104, 162
        positive and negative, 109, 133
        practice of, 161–62
        yunor and, 104, 161
    yunor, 75–77, 89, 90, 107, 156, 159, 161, 176
        attachment and, 107, 133
        and divisions within the self, 133
        dualistic quality, 169
        earth and, 183
        focus and, 75, 78, 104, 108
        freedom and, 77, 88, 107, 123, 133, 134, 156
        freedom and possibility and, 114, 123–25, 133 (*see also*
                freedom: yunor and)
        kav and, 75, 108, 161

    kavek and, 97, 153, 169
    negative, 123
    observing and, 75–78, 80, 88, 97, 104, 107, 108, 133, 134, 143, 169
    positive, 123, 140
    possibility space and, 125, 134
    releasing observation and inner divisions, 97
    support role/support function and, 169
    yune and, 75, 78, 88, 91, 108
    yunem and, 78, 80, 89, 91, 107, 108, 140, 153
    yunoj and, 104, 161
    yunov and, 104, 161
yunor emotions, 133, 140
yunor observing, 77, 78, 80, 83, 86, 88, 108, 159, 169
yunor practice, 75, 86
yunor states, 108
    repression and, 106
yunor thinking, 124, 125
yunov, 108, 140, 161, 164, 178
    depression and, 106, 133, 145, 147
    kavel and, 141, 146
    peace and, 133, 146, 147
    positive and negative, 106–8
    possibilities and, 133, 145, 146
    yune and, 106, 161
    yunor and, 104, 161

Check out Ryan's other projects at:

projectado.com

Join the community at:

depthandconversation.com

Check out Ryan's other books including:

The Mantra of Adoga:
Profound Practices for Personal Growth

&

The Theory and Creation of Music:
A Comprehensive Guide to Composing Your Own Music

www.ingramcontent.com/pod-product-compliance
Lightning Source LLC
Chambersburg PA
CBHW020528080526
44583CB00013B/778